Quilt in a Day®

OHIO ROSE

Yo Yo
page 20

SWEETHEART WREATH

Colonial Knots
page 24

DISTLEFINK

Chain Stitching
page 28

EVENING BLOOMS

Ruching – Miniaturizing Blocks
page 32

BLOCK PARTY VI

Applique in a Day

ELEANOR BURNS

SPRING FLOWERS

Buttercups
page 36

PRESIDENT'S WREATH

Wallhanging
page 40

FRUIT BOWL

Wallhanging
page 44

CHERRY WREATH

Bias Bars
page 48

FLOWER BASKET

Valance
page 52

GRAPE WREATH

Mitering Corners
page 56

HEARTS AND FLOWERS

Fanned Flowers
page 60

HOLLY WREATH

Kwillow
page 64

For Patricia

Thank you for all your help.

Cheerful

Copyright 1994 Eleanor A. Burns Family Trust

ISBN 0-922705-84-4

First Printing   September 1994

Art Direction — Merritt Voigtlander

Graphic Artist — Susan Sells

Photography — Wayne Norton

Spot Illustrations — Debbie Smith

Published by Quilt in a Day®, Inc.

1955 Diamond Street, San Marcos, CA 92069

INTRODUCTION

Traditionally, there are two types of quilts: pieced and appliqued. Easy-to-make pieced quilts were for every day use, while applique quilts were referred to as Best Quilts. They were a challenge to make, and time consuming… so they were often only put out on the guest bed.

We've pieced quilts together from strips, triangles, and squares… all with easy methods since 1978 when I introduced Quilt in a Day Log Cabin. It was revolutionary! Those fast assembly-line methods allowed me the luxury of actually getting quilts finished while raising my two young sons, Grant and Orion.

Now, I'm going to show you how to applique a quilt – with exciting methods I've developed to turn it into an easy quilt for you. And what fun they are! Each beautiful block takes its inspiration and name from nature.

Those traditional hand methods of "needle turn" are still a mystery to me! My secret is turning under the raw edges with fusible interfacing, and heat bonding them in place until the outside edges are stitched down.

Each applique block takes approximately three hours to complete, dividing the process into three steps. First, cut the fabric and sew around each piece, perhaps sewing several blocks at a time. Then bag each block and settle in for a favorite television show, trimming and turning as you watch. It's mindless, relaxing, and may even keep you awake! The final step is to fuse the applique pieces to the background square, and finish the outside edges.

So, can you make a twelve block applique quilt in a day? Not unless the fairies from your garden dig in and help you. But you can easily complete a one block wallhanging in a short day.

Will my applique quilt become my Best Quilt? It's certainly my best, and most exciting year – my fiftieth, and my fiftieth publication to write or edit. That's a landmark you and I have shared!

Beautiful gardens have always reflected on loving and caring hands. Making a quilt also requires those same loving hands. May your quilt be your best, as fresh and beautiful as a tended garden.

Eleanor Burns

FABRIC SELECTION

Yardages are given for:

- ❖ 12 Blocks
- ❖ Setting the Blocks Together
- ❖ Borders

Decide your size and finish in advance, so all of your fabric may be purchased at the same time.

Yardage for 12 Blocks: Pastels or Darker, Richer Colors

Kona Cotton from Robert Kaufman Co., Inc. is the featured fabric, and is referred to by its name. Kona, a quality 100% cotton with a 60 square thread count, is dyed in pure solid colors. Because of its heavy weight, no puckering occurs when machine appliqueing on a single layer of fabric. When Kona Cotton is paired with fusible interfacing, sewn applique pieces are easily turned and shaped.

Yardage for Setting Blocks Together: Lattice and Cornerstones or a Garden Maze setting

Because the Garden Maze setting finishes at 4½" wide and the Lattice and Cornerstone setting at 2½", the overall sizes of the tops are affected. The Lattice and Cornerstone setting is the easier option. If background fabric is used for the Lattice and Cornerstones, the applique patterns appear to float rather than be contained.

Yardage for Borders: Scalloped Border or Floral Border

Either setting does not require a border, but a border may be added to create a larger quilt. The Scalloped Border is the easier of the two. The Floral Border is the equivalent of sewing eight President's Wreath blocks.

Fusible Interfacing

Select non-woven light to medium weight iron-on interfacing. One side of the interfacing is smooth in texture while the other side has fusible dots. **Do not confuse this interfacing with paper backed webbed fusing.**

Fusible interfacing is used to turn under the raw edges of the applique pieces, and fuse them in place without pins.

Various Sizes of Quilts

Yardages are given for a twelve block sampler quilt. You may choose to be creative and make any size quilt. Use these guidelines when planning.

Wallhanging - four block setting (2 x 2)

Twin Size Quilt - eight block setting (2 x 4) plus mitered border

Double Size Quilt - twelve block setting (3 x 4) plus mitered border

Queen Size Quilt - twelve block setting (3 x 4) plus framing border and/or outside border and mitered border

King Size Quilt - sixteen block setting (4 x 4) plus framing border and/or outside border and mitered border

Yardage for the 12 Blocks — *Choose Pastel or Dark*

For a **soft pastel quilt**, purchase these
Kona cotton solids or similar colors in prints:

For a **rich dark quilt**, purchase these
Kona cotton solids or similar colors in prints:

Background Fabric for twelve 16" squares

Pastel	Dark
Snow, White or Natural 3 yds	*Snow, White or Natural* 3 yds

Applique Fabric

Pastel	Dark
Sage 1½ yds	*Sage* ¼ yd
Clay and Wheat ⅛ yd of each	*Alpine* 1¼ yds
Maize ⅓ yd	*Clay and Gold* ⅛ yd of each
Woodrose and Blush Pink ¾ yd of each	*Woodrose and Dusty Pink* ⅛ yd of each
Medium Pink and Plum ¼ yd of each	*Crimson and Deep Rose* ⅓ yd of each
Orchid, Lilac and Amethyst ¼ yd of each	*Rose and Plum* ½ yd of each
Iris ⅝ yd	*Amethyst, Purple, Bright Periwinkle and Eggplant* ¼ yd of each
Candy Blue and Copen ¼ yd of each	*Copen* ⅛ yd, *Royal* ¼ yd, *Hyacinth* ⅝ yd

Fusible Interfacing

Pastel	Dark
Fusible Interfacing 3 yds	*Fusible Interfacing* 3 yds

Cotton Batting for lightly stuffing blocks

Pastel	Dark
Batting 1 yd	*Batting* 1 yd

Embellishments

Pastel	Dark
Buttons, Beads	*Buttons, Beads*

Lattice and Cornerstones 54" x 72"   *Garden Maze 62" x 82"*

Yardage for Setting the Blocks Together — *Choose One*

Select Either	*Lattice and Cornerstone Setting*		
	Lattice	1½ yds	(16) 3" x 33" strips
			cut into (31) 3" x 16" strips
	Cornerstones	¼ yd	(2) 3" x 44" strips
			cut into (20) 3" squares

Or	*Garden Maze Setting*		
	Background Maze	1½ yds	(16) 3" x 33" strips and (2) 4" x 44" strips
			cut into (20) 4" squares
			then cut on both diagonals
	Maze	2 yds	(30) 1½" x 33" strips and (8) 2" x 44" strips
			cut into (40) 2" x 3½"
			and (20) 2" x 7½"

Plus	*Additional Fabric for either Setting (no borders)*		
	Backing	4 yds	(2) 2 yd pieces, seamed
	Lightweight Batting (cotton or polyester)	81" x 96"	
	Binding	⅔ yd	(7) 3" x 44" strips

Scalloped Border

Floral Border

Yardage for the Borders — *Choose One*

Select Either

Floral Border   **10" width**

Bias Vines	½ yd	(14) 1⅜" bias strips
Leaves	⅔ yd	
Five Petal Flowers	½ yd	
Bell Flowers	¼ yd each of two different fabrics	
Buds for Bell Flowers	¼ yd	(56) 2" squares
Bows	¼ yd	
Fusible Interfacing	2 yds	

Or

Scalloped Border   **10" width**

Scallops	2 yds
Flowers	¼ yd
Leaves	⅛ yd
Fusible Interfacing	4 yds

Plus

Additional Fabric for either Border

Mitered Border	3 yds	
Framing and/or Outside Border	1 yd	(10) 3" x 44" strips
Backing	6 yds	(2) 3 yd pieces, seamed
Lightweight Batting (cotton or polyester)	90" x 108"	
Binding	1 yd	(10) 3" x 44" strips

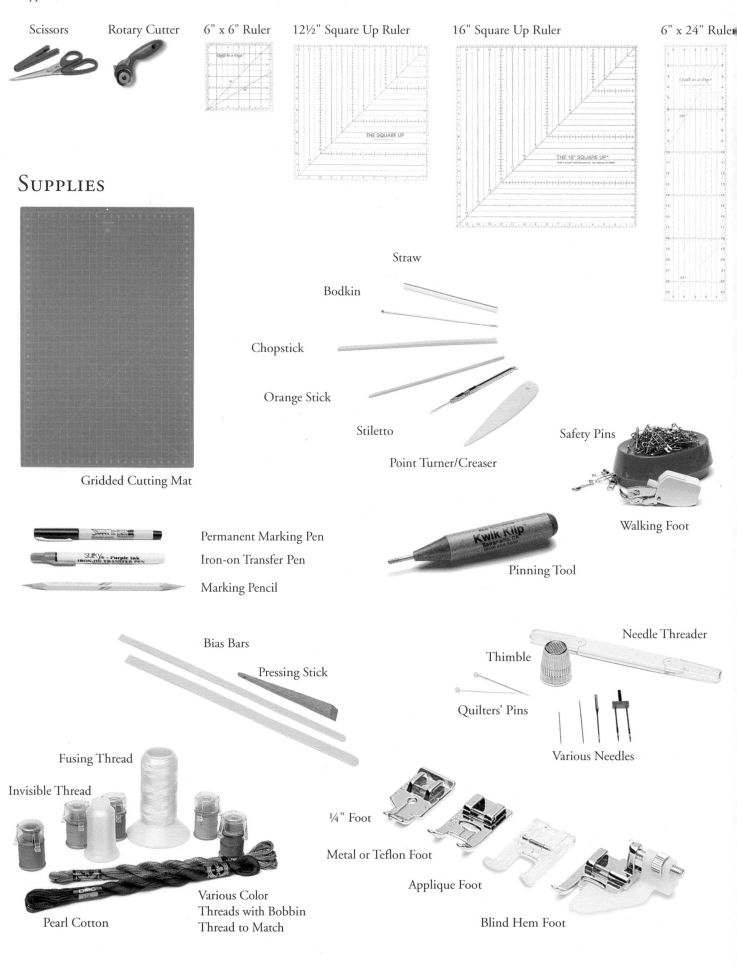

Scissors

Rotary Cutter

6" x 6" Ruler

12½" Square Up Ruler

16" Square Up Ruler

6" x 24" Ruler

SUPPLIES

Gridded Cutting Mat

Straw

Bodkin

Chopstick

Orange Stick

Stiletto

Point Turner/Creaser

Safety Pins

Walking Foot

Permanent Marking Pen

Iron-on Transfer Pen

Marking Pencil

Pinning Tool

Bias Bars

Pressing Stick

Needle Threader

Thimble

Quilters' Pins

Various Needles

Fusing Thread

Invisible Thread

¼" Foot

Metal or Teflon Foot

Applique Foot

Various Color
Threads with Bobbin
Thread to Match

Pearl Cotton

Blind Hem Foot

GENERAL INSTRUCTIONS

Cutting Background Squares

Background squares are 16" square. Only two squares can be cut from a width of fabric, leaving a piece remaining approximately 11" wide. To cut the squares from the fabric, but leave the 11" strip in tact so it's useful later, cut from the selvage edge toward the fold.

Cutting Twelve 16" Background Squares

1. Place the fabric on the gridded cutting mat, folded in half lengthwise. Rest the length of the strip on the table.

2. Place the 16" Square Up ruler just in from the selvage edge.

3. Hold the ruler firm. Rotary cut two sides. Turn the layered squares around, and cut the remaining two sides to a perfect 16".

4. Layer cut twelve 16" background squares. Set the strip from the center fold aside for Garden Maze lattice or borders.

5. Store cut blocks on a skirt hanger.

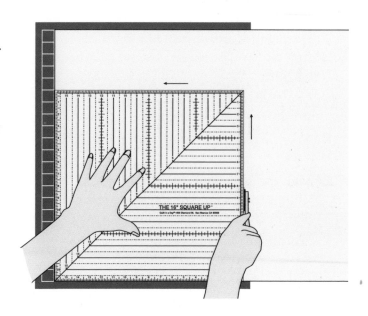

Cutting Smaller Squares and Rectangles for Applique Pieces

Use the 6" Square Up Ruler for pieces smaller than 6", and the 12½" Square Up Ruler for larger pieces.

1. Place the ruler in the lower left corner of the fabric. Move the ruler so the fabric is slightly larger than the given measurement.

2. Rotary cut two sides.

3. Turn the piece, and cut to the exact size.

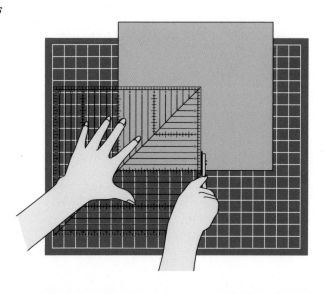

Cutting Strips

1. Fold the fabric in half, selvage to selvage.

2. Straighten the edge.

3. Move your 6" x 24" ruler over until the ruler lines are at the freshly cut edge.

4. Carefully and accurately line up and cut the strips at the measurements given.

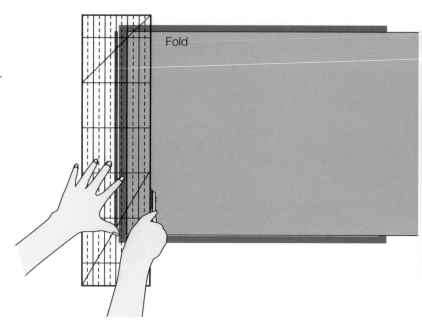

Cutting Garden Maze Lattice Strips

Lattice strips are cut to fit the 16" background squares. Only two strips can be cut from a width of fabric, leaving a piece remaining approximately 11" wide. This strip can be removed first and set aside for later use.

The yardage charts indicate which lattice strips are cut 33" in length.

1. Measure over 33" (2 x 16" plus a little extra). Take a nick in the fabric.

2. Multiply the number of strips times the width of the strips. Tear down this amount plus an extra inch. Tear off this section.

3. Set the remaining 11" fabric strip aside for applique pieces.

4. Cut the 33" strips into the widths specified.

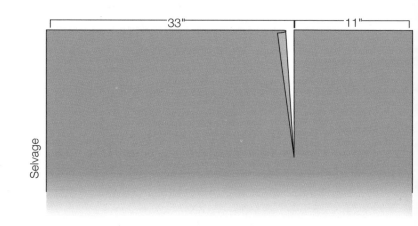

Cutting Border Strips Lengthwise

Borders cut 10" wide are mitered. To allow for the miter, the strips need to be cut 11" longer on each end. Measure your quilt top to determine your lengths.

1. Fold the border fabric in half widthwise, and half again, carefully lining up the selvage edges with the fold.

2. Place on the gridded cutting mat.

3. With the 6" x 24" ruler and rotary cutter, trim off the selvage edges and fold.

4. Cut 10" wide strips lengthwise to your calculated measurements with the 12½" Square Up Ruler.

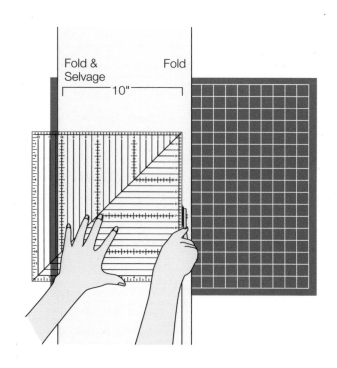

Cutting Bias Strips

Several blocks require bias strips. Cherry Wreath - page 48
Flower Basket - page 52
Hearts and Flowers - page 60 *Optional*

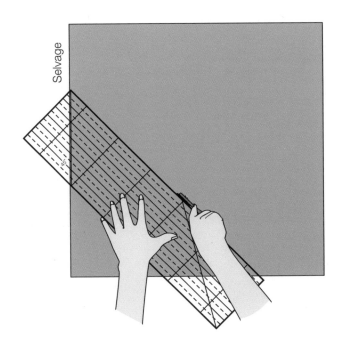
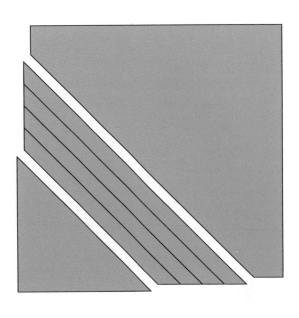

It's best to select these fabrics first, and cut the bias strips before the fabric is cut into other pieces.

1. Line up 45° line on the 6" x 24" ruler with selvage edge of fabric.

2. Cut on 45° angle, or bias. Trimmed piece can be used in other applique.

3. Lining up ruler with the bias, cut the width and number of strips needed.

Cutting the Fusible Interfacing

Fusible Interfacing is generally 22" wide. The twelve patterns have been designed so two patterns (11" x 17" each) fit across the width of the interfacing, and thus are convenient for tracing.

1. Cut into (6) 17" x 22" pieces.

2. Cut each piece in half into (12) 17" x 11" pieces.

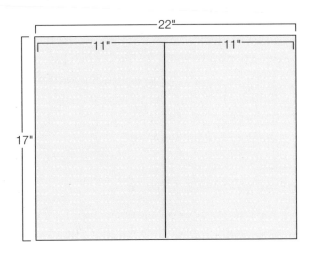

Included for each Block

Instructions are included for twelve different applique blocks. Each block has a:

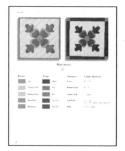

Materials Chart

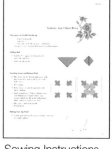

Sewing Instructions

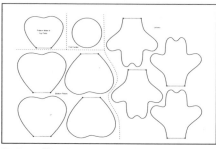

Pattern Sheet

Placement Sheet

Using the Pattern Sheet

Applique pieces are sewn from patterns marked on fusible interfacing. You may

❖ trace the patterns, or

❖ purchase patterns preprinted.

Tracing Patterns onto Fusible Interfacing

1. Remove the pattern sheet for the appropriate block from the book, and unfold. The placement sheet is on the opposite side.

2. Feel the interfacing. Find the smooth side and the "dotted" side. The patterns are traced on the smooth side. The textured "dotted" side is the fusible side.

3. Check the permanence of your pen by drawing on the smooth side of scrap interfacing and steam pressing the dotted side of interfacing to scrap fabric. Substitute pen if it "runs" when pressed.

4. Place an 11" x 17" piece of fusible interfacing on the pattern sheet with the smooth side up.

5. Trace all pieces with a fine, permanent pen. Include the dots and dashed lines.

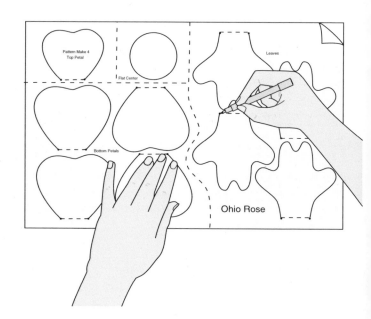

Purchasing Preprinted Patterns

Patterns already conveniently preprinted on fusible interfacing are available for your purchase from Quilt in a Day or your local quilt shop.

Using the Materials Chart

1. Cut the interfacing apart on the long dashed lines.

2. Place each interfacing piece on each corresponding fabric piece with the dotted side against the right side of the fabric. The smooth side of interfacing is on the top.

3. Cut the fabric the same size as the interfacing.

4. If including optional cotton batting for dimension, place underneath the fabric. Explanation follows.

5. Pin in the center of each pattern piece.

Do not press.

Do not press.

Adding Optional Cotton Batting

Light dimension can be added to specified applique pieces by "stuffing" or padding them with cotton batting. Since pieces are pressed after being "stuffed," cotton batting has to be used as polyester will melt and compress.

Use one of these two methods:

❖ Place cotton batting underneath the layered fabric and fusible interfacing. Sew three layers together, trim, and turn. This method is the quicker, but edges tend to be bulky.

❖ Stuff "cut to size" cotton batting inside applique pieces after they are sewn, trimmed, and turned.

Using the Sewing Instruction Sheet

Setting Up your Sewing Machine

1. Select a straight stitch and center needle position on your sewing machine.

2. Use an "open" metal foot or teflon foot for visibility. A clear plastic foot tends to pucker the fusible interfacing at this step.

3. Thread with neutral thread on top and in the bobbin. If you do not have balanced tension, use thread to match the fabric.

4. Set your machine with a tight stitch, 20 stitches per inch or 1.8 to 1.5 on computerized sewing machines.

5. If available, use the "needle down" feature. The needle stops in the fabric each time you stop sewing. This feature makes it easy to control sewing on curves and pivoting.

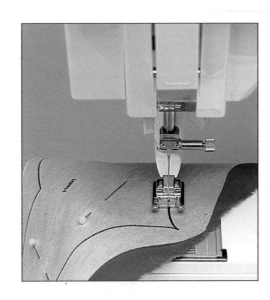

Sewing Around Each Pattern Piece

1. Begin sewing in the middle of a side. Sew on the inside edge of the lines to avoid dark marker lines around the turned pieces.

   If the interfacing puckers, lighten the pressure on the presser foot.

2. Sew slowly on curved pieces, lifting the presser foot and turning the pieces as necessary. Pivot with the needle in the fabric.

3. End by overlapping stitches.

4. Backstitch at dots and leave open as indicated by dashed lines.

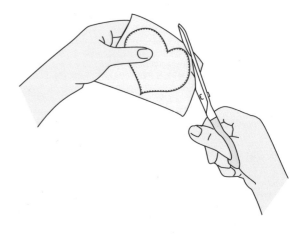

Trimming Each Piece

1. Trim each piece to ⅛" from the lines. Stitching lines are easily seen from the fabric side.

2. Trim corners, and clip inside points.

3. If optional batting was included, trim from the seam by turning scissors sideways.

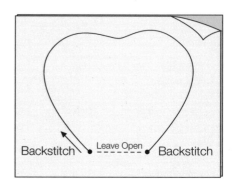

Turning Each Piece

1. Turn pieces marked with two dots through the opening.

2. If the pattern indicated no opening, pull the fusible interfacing away from the fabric.

3. Carefully cut a slit through the fusible interfacing only.

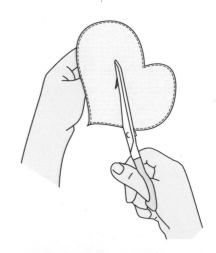

4. With your fingers, carefully turn right side out. From the inside, use the point turner/seam creaser to gently push out curves.

5. From the right side, gently pull out points with stiletto.

6. *Optional:* If pieces have spread open, lightly whipstitch the interfacing together.

   Do not press.

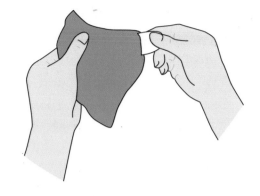

Second Optional Method of Stuffing

1. Using the turned piece as a pattern, cut cotton batting pieces the same shape, but slightly smaller.

2. Insert batting through opening.

3. Smooth edges. An orange stick is useful for this step.

Turning Narrow Applique Pieces

Handy tools to use are a bodkin and collection of different sizes of straws, or plastic tubing, from ¼" to ½" in diameter. Cut the straw or tube ½" shorter than the bodkin. These techniques are especially useful for turning leaves on the Distlefink block and bow ties on the Sweetheart Wreath.

1. Insert large straw into narrow pieces with openings.

2. With the bodkin on the fabric, gently push the narrow piece into the straw.

3. Push the bodkin through the straw, turning the piece at the same time. Remove the straw and bodkin.

4. Turn wider pieces over the bodkin, as the bow on Sweetheart Wreath.

5. For pieces without openings, cut a small slit in interfacing, and turn half at a time.

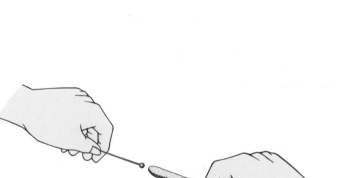

Fingerpressing Under the Interfacing

Do not use the iron on this step.

1. Crease the fabric edges with a pointer/creaser or small wooden "pressing stick," or by "pulling" the edges of the turned piece over the edge of the table.

2. If the fusing has spread open, handstitch closed.

Using the Placement Sheets

Placement sheets are printed on the reverse side of the pattern sheet.

1. Spray the 16" background square with starch for body. Press.

2. Center the 16" background square on the placement sheet. Lines should be visible through the background square.

"Chain Stitching" or Outlining by Machine

1. Lightly trace any lines, as the stems and crest on Distlefink, or vines on Spring Flowers. Extend lines under applique pieces ½".

2. Cut a piece of pearl cotton twice as long plus several inches more than the line.

3. Match the thread to the pearl cotton, or use invisible thread on top and matching thread in the bobbin.

4. Set the machine stitch length at 2 for a small, tight outline stitch, and 3 stitch length for a long, open outline stitch.

5. Place paper under marked background square as a stabilizer. "Junk mail" makes a great stabilizer.

6. Place the center of the pearl cotton on one end of the line.

7. Stitch back and forth over the pearl cotton to anchor it. Use the "needle down" feature on your sewing machine. If unavailable, hand turn the needle so it is in the fabric.

8. Pull the pearl cotton across the presser foot.

9. Hold the ends of the pearl cotton taut.

10. Take 3 machine stitches. Stop with the needle in the fabric. Handturn if necessary. Computer sewing machines can be programmed to stop every 3 stitches.

11. Criss-cross the pearl cotton in front of the needle.

12. Stitch over the pearl cotton, and take 3 machine stitches.

13. Stop with the needle in the fabric, and criss-cross the pearl cotton again.

14. Continue to stitch and criss-cross until the line is covered. Backstitch.

15. If the ends are going to be covered with applique pieces, trim short.

    If ends are not going to be covered, pull to the back side with a needle threader or large eyed needle, tie in a knot, and trim.

16. Perforate the "junk paper" by removing the thread from the needle, and sewing on the "chain stitch" with a very small stitch.

17. Pull the paper away.

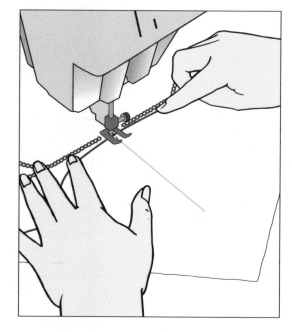

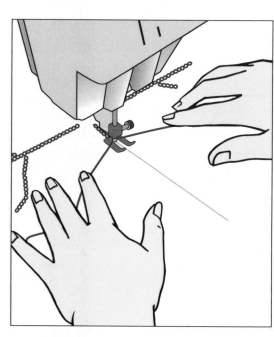

Pressing the Pieces in Place

1. Center the placement sheet on the ironing board or electronic press.

2. Center the 16" background square on the placement sheet.

3. Position pieces on the background square, following the outline of the placement sheet underneath. Tuck raw edges under finished pieces.

4. Carefully slide the placement sheet from under the background square. Be careful not to touch the ink on the paper with iron.

5. Place a pressing cloth over block to prevent possible scorching and dirt from the iron.

6. Using a cotton setting and steam, firmly press pieces to the background. Misting with water also helps pieces fuse. Once they fuse, turn over and press from back side. "Stuffed pieces" may refuse to bond. If so, pin after attempted pressing.

   If you are not satisfied with any placement, peel the piece off, reposition, and press again. Marked edges can be coaxed under with a stiletto. Edge markings can also be pinned under and stitched over later.

Use the 16" ruler under the background square as a base to carry positioned pieces to the iron or press.

A Teflon ironing board cover or a sheet of aluminum foil placed under background squares traps the heat and makes adhering easier.

When using the electronic press, position half of the block at a time and press.

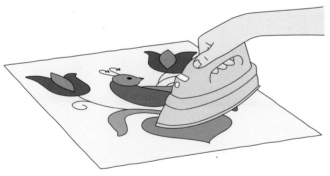

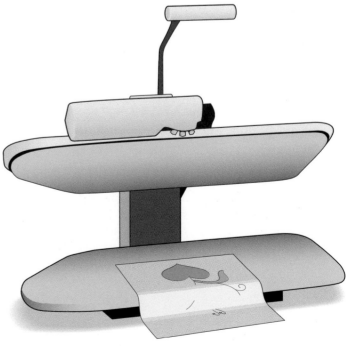

Finishing the Outside Edges

Outside edges of applique pieces can be finished in a variety of ways. Select your favorite method, based on your type of sewing machine.

- ❖ **Straight stitch**
- ❖ **Blind hem or zig-zag stitch**
- ❖ **Decorative machine stitch**

Try out stitches by sewing through several layers of fabric. As you experiment, pencil the stitch selection # or cam # by the stitches. Once you decide on a stitch, record its width and length.

If your fabric puckers while practicing, stabilize the background square by placing a piece of paper under the block. "Junk mail" is a perfect "stabilizer." Tear away the "stabilizer" once the stitching is completed.

Finishing with a Straight Stitch

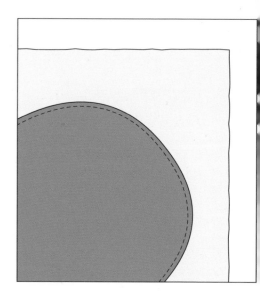

1. Set up your machine top thread with regular, embroidery, topstitching, or hand quilting thread. Select a matching or contrasting color. Use a #70 needle for regular and embroidery thread, and a #90 needle for topstitching and hand quilting thread.

2. Match the color of your regular bobbin thread with your top thread.

3. Set your stitch length #2 to #3. Tighten the top tension for topstitching thread. Adjust the length for each particular piece. Use a small stitch, or 2, for pieces as leaves for curves. Use #3 for larger pieces, as flowers.

4. Line up the inside edge of the presser foot with the edge of the applique piece.

5. Stitch around each piece ¹⁄₁₆" from the edge. Pull the thread at the beginning and end to the wrong side with a needle threader, and knot. Clip the threads.

Finishing with Invisible Thread and a Blind Hem or Zig-zag Stitch

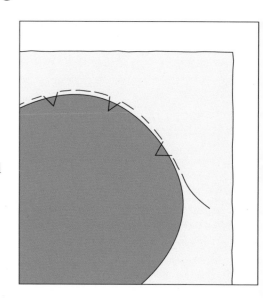

The blind hem stitch can "bite" to the left or right. A narrow zig-zag stitch can also be used. With this technique, the stitches are "invisible."

1. Set up your machine with nylon invisible thread on the top. Loosen your top tension. Use a small, or #70 needle.

2. Load the bobbin with neutral thread to match the background square.

3. Set your stitch length at #2 or 15 stitches per inch and stitch width at 1½.

4. At the end of each piece, overlap the stitching, set your stitch width and length to "0", and stitch in place. Clip the threads.

Blind Hem Stitch

If the stitch "bites" to the right, begin stitching on the left side of the applique piece.

If the stitch "bites" to the left, begin stitching on the right side of the applique piece.

Position the needle so the straight stitches line up with the edge on the background fabric, and the blind hem catches the edge of the applique.

Zig-zag Stitch

The zig-zag should catch both the fabric and the background square.

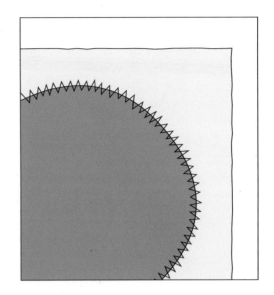

Finishing with Decorative Stitches

The machine stitch that duplicates the look of antique, hand-sewn quilts is the blanket stitch.

1. Select a coordinating or contrasting thread to outline each applique. Use regular or heavy thread in the top and regular thread in the bobbin.

2. Experiment with the blanket stitch, or another one you prefer. A suggested stitch length is #3 with a stitch width of #5.

3. Adjust the stitch so that the straight stitch lines up with the applique on the background fabric, and the "bite" is into the applique.

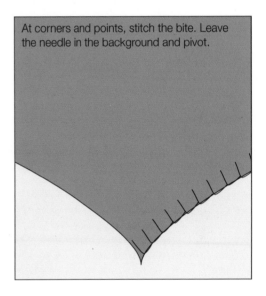

At corners and points, stitch the bite. Leave the needle in the background and pivot.

If the blanket stitch "bites" to the right, begin sewing on the left side of the applique.

If the blanket stitch "bites" to the left, begin sewing on the right side of the applique. Some computerized sewing machines have the capability to "mirror" the stitch, and "bite" in the opposite direction.

Depending on your type of machine, there may be other interesting stitches to finish the outside edge.

The feather stitch adds a decorative touch to leaves and flowers.

≡ ≡ ≡ ≡ ≡ ≡

The topstitch, or triple stitch, is perfect for stems on fruit and tendrils. (See stitch sewn on Grape Wreath, page 57.)

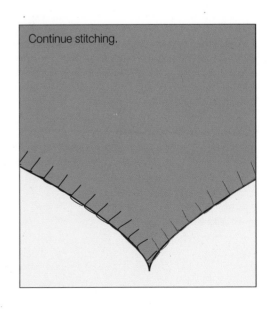

Continue stitching.

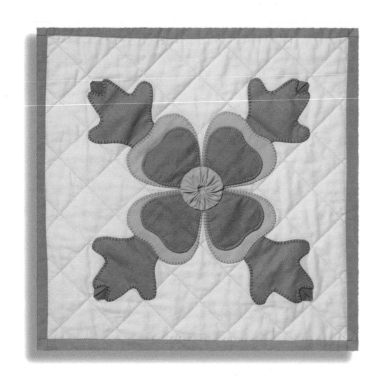

MATERIALS

PASTEL		DARK		APPLIQUE	FABRIC AMOUNT
	Sage		Alpine	**Leaves**	8½" x 11"
	Medium Pink		Rose	**Bottom Petals**	8" x 9"
	Medium Pink		Rose	**Center Circle**	5" square
	Blush Pink		Deep Rose	**Top Petals**	3½" x 30" 3½" x 15" cotton batting *Optional*
	Blush Pink		Deep Rose	**Buds**	(4) 1½" squares

SEWING THE OHIO ROSE

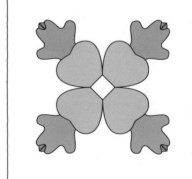

Trace pieces on Fusible Interfacing:

- four bottom petals
- four leaves
- flat center circle (if you choose a flat look)

Sew pieces, trim, and turn following General Instructions.

Folding Buds

1. Fold the 1½" squares on diagonal with right sides out. Press.

2. Fold each side in. Press.

Finishing Leaves and Bottom Petals

1. Place leaves on 16" background square with placement sheet underneath. Center buds under leaves.

2. Press in place.

3. If necessary, coax interfacing under with stiletto and pin.

4. Stitch around leaves. When stitching curves with blind hem or blanket stitch, stop sewing with the needle in the background fabric, and turn, nearly every stitch.

5. Place, press, and stitch around bottom petals.

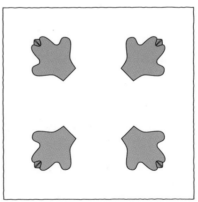

Making Four Top Petals

1. Cut the pattern from the master, or make your own on template plastic.

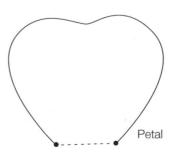

Petal

2. Cut the 3½" x 30" strip in half lengthwise.

3. On wrong side, trace four petals. Remember to leave ½" between petals.

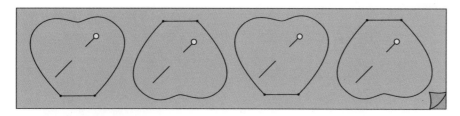

4. Layer right sides together with second half of strip and optional batting for dimension.

5. Sew on lines, trim, and turn. Lightly stuff with cotton batting now if not stitched in seams earlier.

6. Position on the bottom petals. Sew across the open ends.

7. Stitch around flat petals. Padded petals may be stitched or left loose.

Making a Flat Center Circle

1. Layer the fabric with the fusible interfacing pattern. Do not use batting.

2. Sew around the outside edge, trim, and turn.

3. Press in place, and stitch around the outside edge.

Making a Yo Yo Center Circle by Hand

1. Cut a circle with a 4½" diameter from the fabric.

   A circle template is handy for drawing circles with diameters 1¼" to 3½". Use a compass or an assortment of plastic lids for drawing circles larger than 3½".

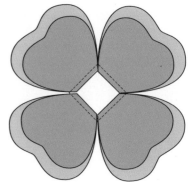

2. Double thread a hand sewing needle with quilting thread or regular matching thread. Knot the end.

3. Sew circle into a yo yo by turning under the edge ¼" to the wrong side, and basting. Pull tight, push the needle to the back, and knot.

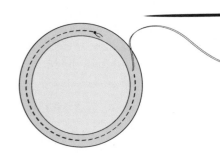

4. Attach to the center of the block with invisible thread and a bar tack stitch, or stitch around the outside edge.

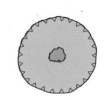

Making a Yo Yo by Machine

A yo yo can be sewn by machine. Load the bobbin with hand quilting thread, lengthen the stitch, and loosen the tension. Sew around the outside edge and gather by pulling on the bobbin thread. Cover the raw edges in the center with a button.

Wallhanging

Pearl Pereira

29" square

Pearl Pereira miniaturized the Ohio Rose by shrinking the pattern to 79%. She set all four rose patterns on whole cloth rather than making individual blocks. Echo quilting and free motion quilting completed this stunning wallhanging.

Quilted Bag

Toni de la Garza

Toni de la Garza designed a bag and embellished it with the Ohio Rose pattern.

Materials

- Pre-quilted background fabric
  1 yard, cut into:
     (1) 18" x 34" piece for bag
     (2) 7½" x 28" pieces for handles
- Blue binding
     (1) 2½" x 40" strip

1. Position and sew applique on right side of quilted fabric.

2. Fold handle pieces in half lengthwise, wrong sides together. Press in half again. Pin. Edgestitch both long sides.

3. Turn under 1" on each end of handle, and sew to inside of bag.

4. Fold bag lengthwise right sides together. Sew both side seams.

5. Pinch the bottom side seams, forming a gusset, and sew across the bottom of both sides. Tack to inside seam.

6. Attach binding to raw edge.

MATERIALS

PASTEL		DARK		APPLIQUE	FABRIC AMOUNT
	Sage		Sage	**Four Leaves**	3½" x 5"
	Sage		Alpine	**Six Leaves**	5½" x 5"
	Woodrose Maize		Eggplant	**Five Petal Flowers**	3½" x 17" or 3½" x 10" and 3½" x 7" 3½" x 17" cotton batting *Optional*
	#445		#781	**Stitched Centers**	DMC Pearl Cotton 3
	Iris		Hyacinth	**Foxgloves**	3" x 10"
	Candy Blue		Plum	**Bow and Ties**	7½" x 7½" 7½" x 4½" cotton batting *Optional*
	Iris		Eggplant	**Center Strip for Bow**	1½" x 4"

SEWING THE SWEETHEART WREATH

Trace pieces on Fusible Interfacing:

- ❖ bow and ties
- ❖ four foxgloves
- ❖ ten leaves (one or two different fabrics)
- ❖ five petal flowers

Sew pieces, trim, and turn following General Instructions. *Optional* Lightly stuff five petal flowers and bow.

Turning the Ties

1. Insert a straw into the open end.
2. Push a bodkin against the "pointed end" of fabric.
3. Turn right side out over the bodkin.

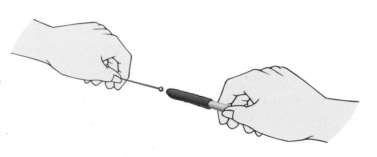

Finishing the Bow

1. Center Strip: Fold the long edges to the center in thirds. Press.
2. Wrap center strip around bow, gathering slightly.
3. Hand tack center strip on back side.

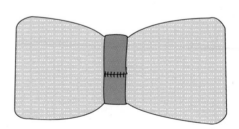

Finishing the Foxglove

Select one of these options:

- ❖ Press flat.
- ❖ Press with fullness in center.
- ❖ Thread a needle with matching thread and knot. From wrong side, insert the needle at one dot, and run a gathering stitch along line to next dot. Draw the gathers up to 1¼", and knot.

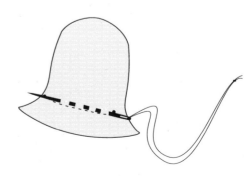

Finishing the Sweetheart Wreath

1. Position bow, ties, and leaves on background square, and press.

2. Finish edges as desired.

3. Position and press foxglove and five petal flowers. Press from wrong side if necessary.

4. Finish edges as desired. Do not sew across bottom of foxglove.

5. *Optional* Embellish base of foxglove with buttons and top of foxglove with green colonial knots.

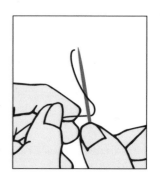

Making Centers for Five Petal Flowers

Select one of these options:

- ❖ Sew three colonial knots to centers. Stitch accent lines from center out.
- ❖ Sew buttons or yo yos to centers.

Colonial Knots

1. Knot pearl cotton and stitch from back side.

2. Lay pearl cotton over fingers, palm up.

3. Put needle over top of pearl cotton on left side. Come up under it to right side.

4. With left hand, wrap thread over needle, left over right, to form a figure eight. The tighter the thread is pulled, the tighter the knot.

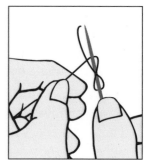

5. Hold thread tight, and push needle to wrong side next to thread's entry point.

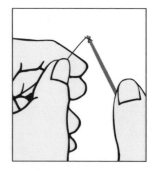

Wallhanging

Janice Orr

21" square

Janice Orr combined solids with a romantic print for her Sweetheart Wreath Wallhanging. The pieces were machine quilted with a blind hem stitch using invisible thread. Framed in two borders, it was finished with a "quick turn" and "stitched in the ditch."

Block

Tecla Miceli

Suitable for a wedding quilt wallhanging, a monogram could be included in the center of the Sweetheart Wreath. For her stylized free motion machine embroidered monogram, Tecla Miceli used rayon machine embroidery thread and a satin stitch. A #60 cotton machine embroidery thread could also be used.

Other methods of monogramming include:

❖ Hand embroidery
❖ Calligraphy using a Pigma pen
❖ Machine writing

Words can be traced onto the background square using a light box. Any words should be sketched onto the background before appliqueing the pieces.

MATERIALS

PASTEL		DARK		APPLIQUE	FABRIC AMOUNT
	Plum		Crimson	**Heart**	5½" x 7½"
	Sage #502		Alpine #501	**Leaves**	5½" x 6" (4) 18" pieces DMC Pearl Cotton 3
	Blush Pink		Eggplant	**Tulips**	5½" x 8½"
	Woodrose		Plum	**Tulip Centers**	3" x 5½" 3" x 5½" cotton batting *Optional*
	Candy Blue		Copen	**Bird Head and Wings**	4" x 5½" 4" x 5½" cotton batting *Optional*
	Copen #322		Royal #312	**Bird Body**	4½" x 11" (2) 20" pieces DMC Pearl Cotton 3
	Maize		Gold	**Beak**	1" square

Optional button or bead for eye

SEWING THE DISTLEFINK

Trace pieces on Fusible Interfacing:

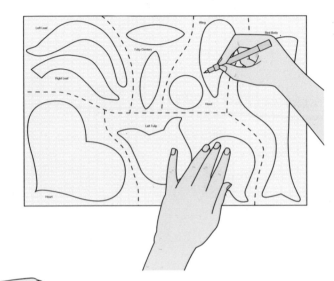

- ❖ leaves
- ❖ bird
- ❖ heart
- ❖ tulips

Sew pieces, trim and turn, following General Instructions.

Optional Lightly stuff tulip centers, wing, and head.

Turning the Leaves

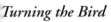

1. Leaf with open end: Insert straw in opening. Turn right side out with bodkin.

2. Leaf without opening: Cut small slit in center back of interfacing. Insert straw in one half of leaf. Turn right side out with bodkin. Insert straw in second half. Turn.

Turning the Bird

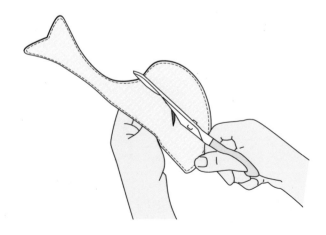

1. Make small slit in fusible interfacing.

2. Insert plastic tube or straw into tail. Turn right side out by pushing on fabric with bodkin.

3. Turn body with fingers.

4. Pull out the tail from the right side with the stiletto.

5. Whipstitch opening.

"Chain Stitching" the Stems

1. Place the 16" background square on the placement sheet.

2. Trace stems and bird's crest. Extend ends of lines ½" under the applique pieces.

3. "Chain stitch" curved stem first. * Pull pearl cotton ends to backside with a large needle or needle threader, and knot.

4. "Chain stitch" remaining stems, backstitch over the ends, and trim. Pearl cotton ends are covered later.

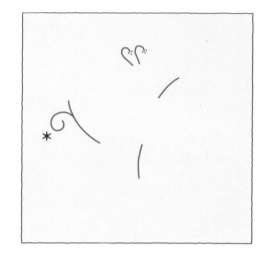

Making the Beak

1. Fold 1" square in half, wrong sides together, and press.

2. Press again on diagonals.

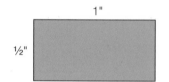 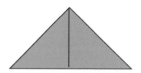

Finishing the Distlefink

1. Place pieces on 16" background square in alphabetical order:

2. Tuck beak under head.

3. Press in place.

4. Sew around each piece as desired.

5. Starting at the head, "chain stitch" the bird's crest. Do not clip the pearl cotton. Make colonial knots at end of crest. See page 26.

6. Sew on a bead or button for eye, or make a colonial knot eye.

Wallhanging

Anne Dease

25" square

Anne Dease chose solid primary colors for this charming Distlefink Wallhanging, carrying the theme with the bright floral Garden Maze border.

Both the primary colors and the Distlefink pattern are popular with children. Five year old Elyse Dobrick delightfully commented, "I like the birdie bird!"

Vest

Lou Short

Lou Short's Distlefink makes an eye catching decoration in rich prints for the back of her ready-to-wear vest. Instead of tulips, she took the liberty of using five petal flowers with yo yo centers topped with pearl heart buttons. The pieces are hand appliqued in place with a blanket stitch using embroidery floss.

Sweatshirt

Pearl Pereira

Pearl Pereira turned a ready-to-wear sweatshirt into a one-of-a-kind garment with the Distlefink pattern using bright prints. She machine appliqued the pieces in place with invisible thread.

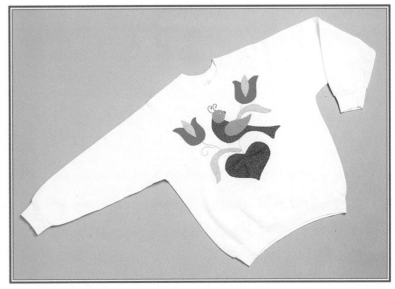

MATERIALS

PASTEL		DARK		APPLIQUE	FABRIC AMOUNT
	Medium Pink		Deep Rose	**Six Evening Lilies**	6½" x 9" 6½" x 9" cotton batting *Optional*
	Blush Pink		Rose	**Chrysanthemum**	1¾" x 30" 36" heavy string
	Sage		Alpine	**Four Leaves**	6" x 6"
	Maize		Gold	**Blossoms**	(2) circles with 2¼" diameter
	Sage		Alpine	**Two Calyxes and Fourteen Leaves**	4½" x 15"
	#502		#501	**Vines**	(2) 1½ yds. pieces DMC Pearl Cotton 3

Sewing the Evening Blooms

Trace pieces on Fusible Interfacing:

- ❖ six evening lilies
- ❖ four leaves
- ❖ two calyxes, fourteen leaves

Sew pieces, trim, and turn following General Instructions. *Optional* Lightly stuff lilies.

Outlining the Vines

1. Lightly trace the "chain stitch" lines.
2. "Chain stitch" one half of the vine at a time. Backstitch and trim pearl cotton. Pearl cotton ends are covered later.

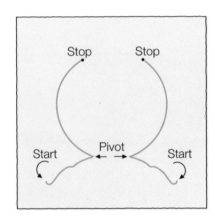

Sewing Blossoms

1. Fold circles in half, wrong sides together.
2. Baste around outside edge of each half circle.
3. Pull tight. Arrange with gathers across bottom.
4. Knot off.

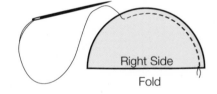

Placing the Pieces

1. Place pieces on background square. Tuck blossoms in the calyxes. Press.
2. Finish outside edges. Straight stitching around four leaves and evening lilies is attractive.
3. Referring to the pattern, sew dimensional lines on evening lilies.

Making the Chrysanthemum with "Ruching"

1. Fold the 1¾" x 30" strip in half lengthwise with right sides together.

2. Knot the end of the string, and place against the fold.

3. Backstitch, and stitch with 15 stitches per inch and ¼" seam allowance. Trim long side to ⅛".

4. Turn right side out by pulling on string. Press strip with seam at center back.

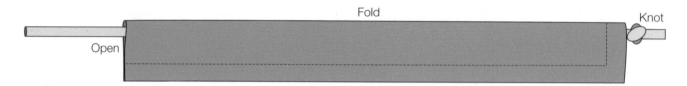

5. Place the end of the strip on the illustration below.

6. Using the illustration as a guide, make small marks on the edge of the strip every 1".

7. Starting at the right end of the strip, knot, and stitch with quilting thread or matching regular thread from dot to dot. Take a stitch over the folded edge each time you change direction. This can also be sewn by machine. Load the bobbin with machine quilting thread, and loosen the tension.

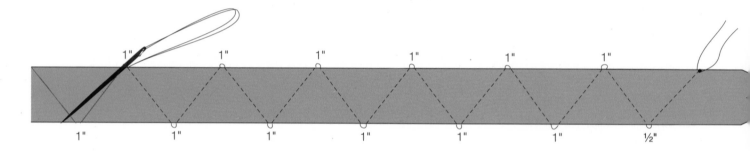

8. If hand sewing, stitch several inches and pull, gathering the fabric on both sides.

9. Stitch to the end, gathering to 15". Adjust the fabric petals. Knot off.

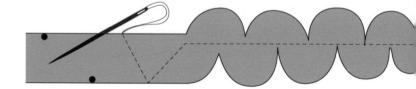

10. Baste across the bottom of the first six petals, pull into a circle, and sew together.

    You can complete the chrysanthemum by hand or machine. When sewing by hand, use matching thread and stitch on the wrong side. When sewing by machine, use invisible thread in the top, matching thread in the bobbin, and bar tack from the right side.

11. Arrange seventh petal under sixth, and wrap second row behind circle. Continuously arrange and stitch.

12. Wrap the end underneath, and knot off.

13. Hand or machine sew the chrysanthemum to the center of the four leaves. Tack as desired.

14. *Optional* Sew colonial knots in center of chrysanthemum. See page 26.

Wallhanging

Brenda Stout Applegate

23" square

Brenda Stout Applegate combined solids and a print in her elegant Victorian Evening Blooms Wallhanging. She hand appliqued with a blind applique stitch using a fine needle and regular thread to match the pieces. For variety, Brenda used 1 strand of light green and 1 strand of dark green pearl cotton for colored stems. The mitered border is overlaid with an appliqued scallop.

Materials

- ❖ Fusible interfacing
  (4) 2½" x 22" strips
- ❖ Green fabric for the scallop
  (4) 2½" x 22" strips
- ❖ Floral fabric for border
  (4) 4" x 24" strips

Using the pattern, trace the scallops onto the 4 strips of 2½" x 22" fusible interfacing. Pin fusible interfacing on green fabric, and sew on the traced scallop line. Trim, clip corners, and turn. Center and press the scalloped borders to the 4" floral borders. Finish scallop edge by hand or machine. *Instructions for mitered borders are found on page 59.*

Carefully line up the scallops when completing the mitered border.

Wallhanging

Pearl Pereira

32" square

Pearl Pereira miniaturized the Evening Blooms by shrinking the pattern to 79%. She arranged the four patterns on point to form a circle on whole cloth rather than four individual blocks. She machine quilted the pieces using clear invisible thread and a blind hem stitch.

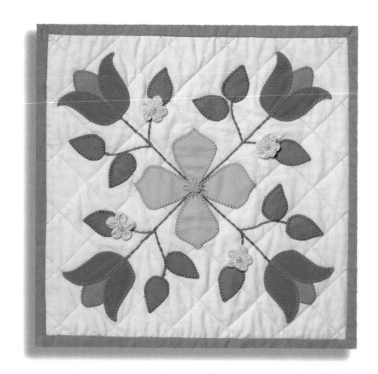

MATERIALS

PASTEL		DARK		APPLIQUE	FABRIC AMOUNT
	Sage		Alpine	**Leaves**	4" x 17" 4" x 17" cotton batting *Optional*
	Medium Pink		Rose	**Dogwood**	5" x 8½" 5" x 8½" cotton batting *Optional* 1 yd. DMC Pearl Cotton 3
	Copen		Royal	**Outside Tulip Petals**	7" x 9" 7" x 9" cotton batting *Optional*
	Candy Blue		Copen	**Inside Tulip Petals**	4" x 9"
	Maize		Gold	**Buttercups**	(4) circles with 3½" diameter (4) small buttons or pearls for centers *Optional*
	#502		#501	**Vine**	(8) 18" pieces DMC Pearl Cotton 3

SEWING THE SPRING FLOWERS

Trace pieces on Fusible Interfacing:

- ❖ leaves
- ❖ dogwood
- ❖ tulips

Sew pieces, trim, and turn following General Instructions.

Turn inside tulip petals with straw and bodkin. See page 25.

Optional Lightly stuff these pieces with cotton batting.

Outlining the Vines

1. Lightly trace the "vine" lines on 16" background square. Be careful not to mark the center under the dogwood.

2. Working on one quarter at a time, "chain stitch" the vines with pearl cotton. *Sew the curved vines from end to end first, and straight vines second using a new piece of pearl cotton each time. Pearl cotton ends are covered later.

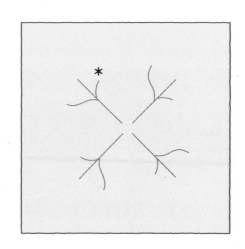

Making the Dogwood

1. Press in place. Stitch around the outside edges.

2. Fill the center with colonial knots. See page 26.

3. Embellish with short stitches around the center.

Making Tulips

1. Press the four inside petals in place.
2. Stitch the top half only.

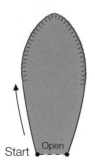

3. Hand whipstitch turning holes on outside petals, and press in place.
4. Continuously stitch around outside edge, beginning in center, and following direction of arrows.
5. Press and stitch the leaves in place.

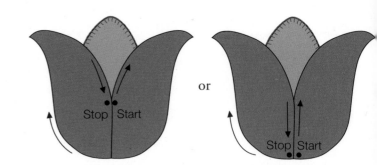

Making Buttercups

1. With hand sewing needle and double thread, sew 3½" circles into yo yos. See page 22. Pull the thread to the center back and knot, but leave threaded needle attached.
2. Place yo yo on this illustration, and mark five division lines around outside edge.

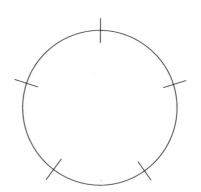

3. Stitching from the back, wrap the thread around the yo yo and pull tight at each mark.

4. Sew to the block, holding in place with stitches or an optional button or bead.

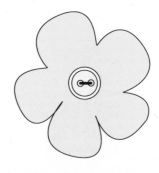

Wallhanging

Lois Litton Thornhill

25" square

Lois Litton Thornhill chose to hand applique the Spring Flowers on her wallhanging. She used "fussy cut" petals for the dogwood, and gave them additional dimension by tacking the centers only. The tulip petals have been given extra dimension by leaving the outer petals free in the center, stitching only where the petals touch the background.

Lois highlighted the whole design with echo quilting. The "crowning glory" is the gold thread hand quilted in the gold design of the fabric.

Fussy Cuts

1. Choose a portion of the print that is the desired shape and size.
2. Trace the pattern on fusible interfacing.
3. Center the interfacing pattern (smooth side up) on the fabric, pin, and cut ½" larger than the pattern. Sew on the lines, trim and turn following the General Instructions.

Hand Applique

1. Thread a sharp or applique needle with 18" of a single strand of regular thread that matches the color of the applique piece.
2. Sew a blind stitch that shows just a tiny spot of thread on the front and a slightly longer stitch on the back:

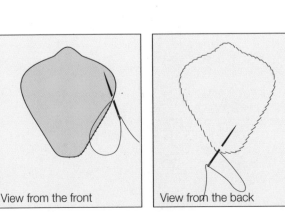

View from the front

View from the back

❖ Bring the thread up through the background fabric and catch just a couple of threads on the fold of the applique. Push the needle down through the background right above the spot where it came up.
❖ Move the needle about ⅛" away, and come up through the background and applique piece again.
❖ Pull the stitches firmly but not too tightly.

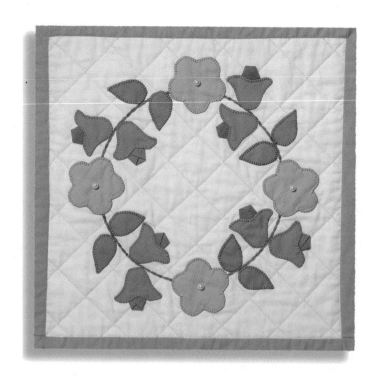

MATERIALS

PASTEL		DARK		APPLIQUE	FABRIC AMOUNT
	Sage		Alpine	**Leaves**	6" x 7" or (2) 3" x 7"
	#502		#501	**Vine**	(4) 18" pieces DMC Pearl Cotton 3
	Iris		Hyacinth	**Bell Flowers**	5½" x 11"
	Blush Pink		Rose	**Buds**	(8) 2" squares
	Woodrose		Plum	**Five Petal Flowers**	4" x 15" 4" x 15" cotton batting *Optional*

buttons or yo yo
centers *Optional*

Sewing the President's Wreath

Trace pieces on Fusible Interfacing:

> ❖ leaves
> ❖ bell flowers
> ❖ five petal flowers

Sew pieces, trim, and turn following General Instructions.

Optional Lightly stuff five petal flowers.

"Chain Stitching" the Vine

1. Place the 16" background square on the placement sheet.
2. Trace the vine from five petal flower to five petal flower, and extend lines ½" on each end.
3. "Chain stitch" each section, backstitch, and trim.
   Pearl cotton ends are covered later.

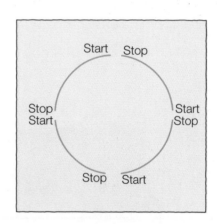

Folding the Buds

1. Fold 2" squares wrong sides together on the diagonal. Press.
2. Fold in the ends. Press.

Arranging the Pieces

1. Place pieces on the background square.
2. Tuck buds under bell flowers.
3. Press in place.
4. Finish outside edges.
5. Embellish centers of five petal flowers with buttons or yo yos.

Wallhanging

Lois Litton Thornhill

39" square

Lois Litton Thornhill adapted the applique technique as an embellishment to a 16 block barn raising Log Cabin Wallhanging. She used 1½" wide strips of one light and a variety of rich, dark strips to make 7" blocks. The scattered applique leaves and buds across the light areas are outline hand quilted. Hand quilting in the dark portion emphasizes the design. The two narrow borders were cut at 1½" and the wide border at 3¾".

Vest

Betty Rossiter

Betty Rossiter's daisy vest is applique embellished with a flower pot, five petal flowers and leaves. Buttons further enhance the individual flowers, and a delicate floral ribbon encircles the vest. The padded front panels are overall machine quilted, giving the garment a textured feel.

Wallhanging

Carol Selepec

33" square

Carol Selepec's President's Wreath block is machine appliqued with a blind hem stitch using invisible thread. Pearl cotton forms the wreath vine.

The block is outlined with a 1" solid lavender border cut from 1½" strips to a make a 17½" block. Additional five petal flowers and leaves embellish the corners. To set the block on point cut two 13" background squares. Cut each on the diagonal for the corner triangles. Cut the first border strips at 1½" wide and the second border strips at 3½".

Cafe Valance

Mackie

40" x 12"

Mackie arranged the applique pieces for her President's Wreath in a long design to enhance a valance of pre-quilted muslin. She added a ready-made piping along the bottom edge to compliment the matching stem.

Materials

- ⅓ yard of 42" wide pre-quilted muslin
- ⅓ yard of 42" wide plain muslin backing
- 42" piping

1. Right sides together, pin muslin and pre-quilted muslin, inserting piping at one long edge.

2. Sew around pieces, leaving 2" unsewn at top of one short side and 6" open at opposite end for turning. The rod will be inserted through these openings.

3. Turn right side out through larger opening. Handstitch to close, leaving 2" open for rod. Turn in the raw edges of the two openings and hand stitch.

4. Applique pieces as desired.

Materials

Pastel		Dark		Applique	Fabric Amount
	Candy Blue		Hyacinth	**Bowl**	4½" x 9½"
	Blush Pink		Crimson	**Strawberries**	3" x 5½"
	Wheat		Clay	**Pear**	2½" x 4"
	Plum		Deep Rose	**Apple**	3½" x 3½"
	Lilac Amethyst		Plum Eggplant	**Plum**	1¼" x 3½" 2" x 3½"
	Clay		Clay	**Fruit Stems**	1¼" x 6"
	Lilac Amethyst Orchid		Amethyst Bright Periwinkle Purple	**Flat or Dimensional Grapes**	(2) 4" squares or (11) circles with 3" diameter
	Maize		Gold	**Pineapple**	4¼" x 6" 4¼" x 6" cotton batting *Optional*
	Sage		Alpine	**Stalks, Grape Leaf and Fruit Leaves**	7" x 10" 7" x 10" cotton batting *Optional*
	Sage		Alpine	**Strawberry Leaves**	(3) 1½" x 2"
	#502		#501	**Tendrils**	DMC Pearl Cotton 3

SEWING THE FRUIT BOWL

Trace pieces on Fusible Interfacing:

- ❖ strawberries
- ❖ pear
- ❖ apple
- ❖ plum
- ❖ flat grapes
- ❖ pineapple — trace dashed lines on interfacing
- ❖ stalk and leaves

Sew two plum strips together. Line up seam with dashed line on pattern piece.

Sew pieces, trim, and turn following General Instructions.

Optional Lightly stuff pineapple and stalk, pear, apple, and grape leaf with cotton batting.

Topstitching the Pineapple

1. Load machine with brown thread.
2. From the interfacing side, sew on the grid lines with a straight stitch and 10 stitches per inch.
3. Pull threads to wrong side, and knot.

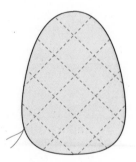

Making the Free-floating Stalk

1. Trace free-floating stalk on template plastic.
2. Fold 2" x 6" piece of fabric in half, right sides together.
3. Trace two patterns with mirror image.
4. Sew on the lines, trim, and turn.

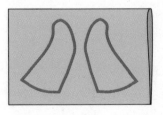

Making Three Fruit Stems

1. Fold the 1¼" x 6" strip in half, right sides together.
2. Sew ⅛" seam across one end and long side. Sew two short seams, and backstitch.
3. Cut apart.
4. Turn over very narrow straw with bodkin.

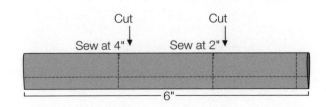

Cut · Cut
Sew at 4" ▼ · Sew at 2" ▼
6"

Making Dimensional Grapes

Sew the 3" circles into yo yos. See page 22.

Positioning Pieces

1. Place pineapple, stalks, and bowl on background, following placement sheet.

2. Press in place.

3. Finish outside edges.

4. Press pear, plum, and apple with stems tucked under. Finish outside edges.

5. Press strawberries and grape leaf in place. Finish outside edges.

6. Press flat grapes in place, and sew around with a straight stitch. Sew dimensional grapes in the center or outside edge.

7. Press remaining leaves in place, and finish outside edges. Topstitch. Leave two short stalks on pineapple loose.

Making Strawberry Leaves

1. Fold 1½" x 2" strips in half lengthwise, right sides together.

2. Assembly-line sew short ends.

3. Turn right side out, and fold.

4. Tuck in ends.

5. With a hand sewing needle, gather and wrap around the center. Stitch to strawberries.

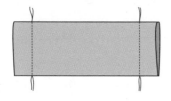

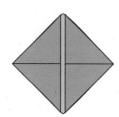

Embellishing the Fruit

Trace and hand or machine outline stitch, or couch with pearl cotton.

- ❖ stems of strawberries
- ❖ tendrils
- ❖ grape leaf

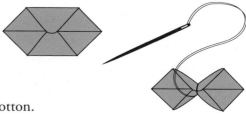

Couching Tendrils by Hand

1. Knot end of pearl cotton and bring up through fabric on end of embellishment line.

2. Arrange pearl cotton in loops and pin through circles.

3. With matching thread, bring up needle on one side of pearl cotton. Stitch across pearl cotton.

Couching Tendrils by Machine

1. Place a cording foot on your sewing machine.

2. Select a blanket stitch.

3. Place the pearl cotton under the foot and stitch, catching the pearl cotton.

4. Sew a tiny zig-zag over ends and trim.

Wallhanging

Ruth Griffith

Pat Wetzel

25" square

Ruth Griffith teamed up with Pat Wetzel to create this bountiful Fruit Basket Wallhanging. The pieces are appliqued in matching thread and outline quilted by machine.

To create a "table effect," cut the background 12½" x 16" and the brown strip 3½" x 16". Insert the doily between the two strips before sewing them together.

To make the pieces quickly for the wallhanging, use paper backed fusible webbing in place of the fusible interfacing. This method works well for wallhangings that won't be laundered.

Paper Backed Fusible Webbing Technique

1. Place the paper backed fusible webbing on the pattern sheet, paper side up. Trace.

2. Cut the fusing apart on the dashed lines.

3. Place the webbed, fusible side on the wrong side of the fabric.

4. Press for 7 seconds.

5. Cut around each piece on the lines.

6. Peel the paper away from the wrong side. If the paper does not peel away easily, wait 24 hours, and try again. "Scoring" the paper with a pin helps release the paper. Trim any frayed edges.

7. Place the pieces on the background. Press in place.

8. Finish the outside edges with a blanket or zig-zag stitch.

MATERIALS

PASTEL		DARK		APPLIQUE	FABRIC AMOUNT
	Plum Blush Pink Woodrose		Deep Rose Woodrose Crimson	**Flat Cherries**	4" x 6" 4" x 6" 4" square 4" x 15" cotton batting *Optional*
	Plum Blush Pink Woodrose		Deep Rose Woodrose Crimson	**or Dimensional Cherries**	(6) circles with 3" diameter (6) circles with 3" diameter (4) circles with 3" diameter
	Sage		Alpine	**Twig Wreath**	22" square
	Sage		Alpine	**Ten Leaves**	7" x 9½" (trimmed piece from wreath)
	Sage		Sage	**Six Leaves**	6" x 7"

SEWING THE CHERRY WREATH

Trace pieces on Fusible Interfacing:

- ❖ flat cherries
- ❖ leaves

Sew pieces, trim, and turn following General Instructions. *Optional* Lightly stuff cherries.

Making Dimensional Cherries

Sew the 3" fabric circles into yo yos. See page 22.

Outlining the Twig Wreath

Lightly trace the wreath on the background fabric.

Making Bias for the Twig Wreath

1. Line up 45° line on 6" x 24" ruler with selvage edge of fabric.

2. Cut on 45° angle, or bias. Use trimmed piece for leaves.

3. Lining up ruler with the bias, cut (4) 1⅜" x 10" bias strips, or a combination of lengths to total 10", and (1) continuous 1⅜" x 27" bias strip.

4. Load bobbin with fusing thread. Thread the top with matching thread. *The fusing thread adheres the bias strip to the background square when pressed.*

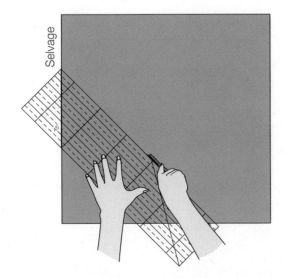

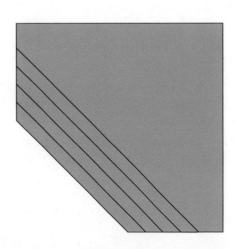

5. Fold bias strips wrong sides together. Sew with a small stitch, 1.8 or 18 stitches per inch, and ¼" seam allowance. The seam must be perfectly straight.

6. Insert ⅜" wide bias bar into strip. On back side, center seam, and finger press seam to one side so fusible thread is exposed.

7. Press flat from the right side. Do not touch fusible thread with iron.

8. Push the bar through the strip, pressing the length of strip.

9. Trim seam to ⅛".

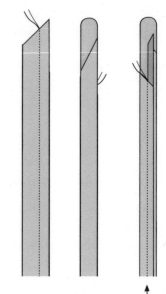

Fusing Thread ⟶

Threading Machine with Twin Needle

The easiest way to consistently topstitch the bias strips is with a 6 mm twin needle, size 100. (6.0/100) Use the twin needle only with a wide zig-zag foot and an extra wide throat plate. Before sewing, carefully hand turn the needles, and check for clearance on the throat plate. Twin needles less than 6 mm apart can be used. In this case make the bias strip narrower.

1. Set stitch width dial to straight stitch, and 12 stitches per inch.

2. Use separate spools of thread for each needle. Thread them separately to each needle.

Twin Needle

Making the Four Corner Twigs

1. Cut each 10" bias strip into (2) 2" pieces and (1) 4" piece.

2. Cut ends of 2" pieces on diagonals to create "miter." With fusible thread on bottom, press in place. Topstitch.

   Be careful when you remove the block from the machine because threads pucker when pulled. Pull and release the threads by hand, and clip. Do not pull fabric.

3. Place 4" piece on top and press in place. Topstitch.

4. Cut end of 27" bias strip straight. Beginning at spot covered later with cherry, position and press bias strip in place. Topstitch.

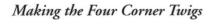

Adding Cherries and Leaves

1. Position cherries and leaves on twig wreath.

   If necessary, cover crooked topstitching with cherries.

2. Sew around the outside edges.

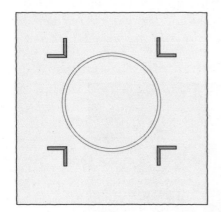

Wallhanging

LuAnn Stout

Luckie Yasukochi

25" x 26"

LuAnn Stout and Luckie Yasukochi combined their talents to make this delightful Cherry Wreath Wallhanging. LuAnn hand appliqued the stems and yo yos. Leaves were machine quilted with matching regular thread using a blanket stitch.

The border has a welting strip for added interest.

Luckie completed the wallhanging with free motion machine quilting in the center of the wreath and four corners.

Materials

❖ Welting fabric
   cut (4) 1" x 21" strips
❖ First border
   cut (4) 1½" wide strips
❖ Second border
   cut (4) 3¼" wide strips

1. Pin and sew on the first border.

2. Fold the welting fabric in half wrong sides together and press.

3. Pin folded welting strips to two opposite sides of the first border with folds toward the quilt, and raw edges matched.

4. Pin welting strips to two remaining sides, overlapping the welting at the corners. Baste.

5. Add the second border, exposing ¼" of welting on the right side.

Free Motion Machine Quilting

Refer to your instruction manual for directions on how to darn with your machine. Use a darning foot or spring needle, and drop or cover your feed dogs with a throat plate.

No stitch length is required as you control the stitch length. Use a fine needle and a little hole throat plate. Use invisible thread in the top and thread to match the backing in the bobbin.

1. Lightly trace the design on the background fabric.

2. Bring the bobbin thread up at the beginning point. Lower the needle into the end of the design and drop the foot. Moving the fabric very slowly, take a few tiny stitches to lock them. Snip off the tails of the threads.

3. With your eyes watching the line ahead of the needle, and your fingertips stretching the fabric and acting as a quilting hoop, move the fabric in a steady motion while the machine is running at a constant speed. Keep the top of the wallhanging in the same position by moving the fabric underneath the needle side to side, and forward and backward.

4. Lock off the tiny stitches and clip the threads at the end of the design.

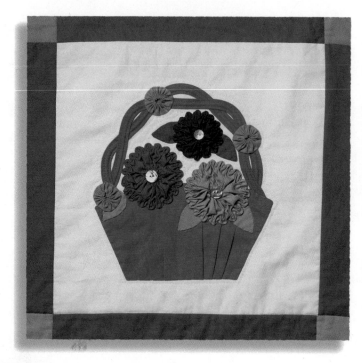

MATERIALS

PASTEL		DARK		APPLIQUE	FABRIC AMOUNT
	Iris		Hyacinth	**Basket**	6½" x 14"
	Iris		Hyacinth	**Handles**	20" square
	Maize Plum Candy Blue		Gold	**Small Flowers**	(3) circles with 3½" diameter (3) buttons or beads *Optional*
	Sage		Sage Alpine	**Leaves**	5½" square
	Maize Blush Pink		Rose Plum	**Large Peony with Ruched Edge**	(1) 2¼" x 20" of each (3) 25" pieces of heavy string
	Woodrose		Eggplant	**Small Peony with Ruched Edge**	2" x 16" (1) 20" piece of heavy string
	Blush Pink Maize Woodrose		Rose Plum Eggplant	**Centers**	(1) circle with 3½" diameter of each or buttons
	Blush Pink Maize Woodrose		Rose Plum Eggplant	**or Five Petal Flowers**	(1) 4" square of each

SEWING THE FLOWER BASKET

Trace pieces on Fusible Interfacing:

> ❖ five petal flowers *Optional These flowers are less dimensional than ruched flowers.*
> ❖ leaves
> ❖ basket (set aside)

Sew optional flower and leaves, trim, and turn following General Instructions.

Making the Basket

1. Place 6½" x 14" fabric strip on pattern guide and mark lines along edges. Working from the center out, fold over and press at the solid lines. Tuck under at the dashed lines.

2. Place the dotted side of the fusible interfacing right sides together to the tucks. Pin.

3. Sew on the lines. Trim and turn following General Instructions.

Making the Handle

1. Trace outline of handles on background square.

2. Line up 45° line on 6" x 24" ruler with edge of fabric. Cut. See pages 49 and 50.

3. Lining up ruler with the bias, cut two 1¾" x 21" bias strips.

4. Fold bias strips wrong sides together. Sew with ¼" seam, small stitch, regular thread on top, and fusing thread in bobbin.

5. Press with ½" wide bias bar. Trim seam to ⅛".

6. Loosely braid handles together as they are shaped and pressed in place on background square.

7. With twin needle and double thread, sew down the center of each handle. For an attractive finish, stitch only on the top braids. Pull back edges of overlapping braids, and stitch to seams. Pull threads to back side at braids.

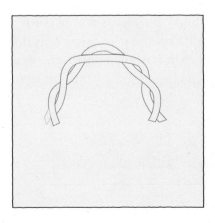

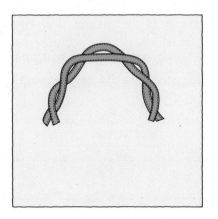

Finishing the Pieces

1. Place basket and optional five petal flowers on background square, and press.

2. Finish outside edges as desired.

Making Small Flowers

Refer to Buttercup instructions on page 38.

Making Ruched Flowers

1. On wrong side, measure in 1" and draw pencil line length of strip. Measure in ¼" on opposite side and draw line.

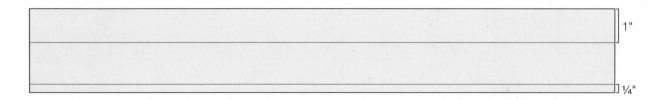

2. Fold raw edge to 1" line, wrong sides together, and press a ½" hem. This edge is the ruching edge.

3. Starting at the right top folded edge, measure in ½" and mark a dot. Continue marking a dot every 1", stopping ½" from the opposite side.

4. Along the bottom edge of fold, measure in 1" and mark a dot every 1".

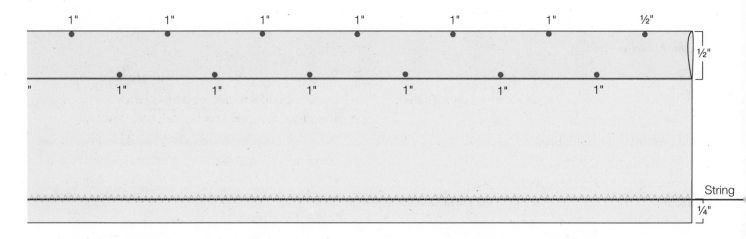

5. Place the string on the ¼" drawn line. With thread matching fabric, machine zig-zag stitch over string. Use a long stitch and wide zig-zag. Thread will be drawn up forming center after ruching is completed.

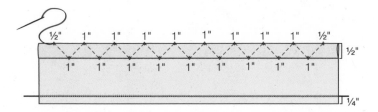

6. Double strand and knot a hand sewing needle with matching thread. Beginning on the right end, hand stitch from dot to dot. At the folded edge, wrap the stitch over fold and continue. Do not cut thread at end.

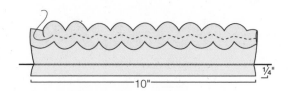

7. Pull gathers and string evenly until the strip measures 10" in length.

8. Fold the two short ends together, and stitch with a ½" seam.

9. Pull string tightly, forming the center of the flower. Tie a square knot, and trim ends of string.

10. Pin flower onto background square and stitch at indentations.

11. Cover the ragged center with a button or yo yo. *Optional* Turn yo yo upside down and stitch.

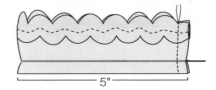

Vest

Nancy Loftis

Nancy Loftis hand appliqued ruched, five petal and yo yo flowers to an easy vest pattern. Centers of the five petal and yo yo flowers are French knots. The basket is topstitched over a pocket on three sides. The top of the basket is whip stitched by hand to the pocket. For extra body, the light-weight cotton vest was interlined with fusible pellon. However, for a heavier vest, the fabric could easily be quilted in a grid design before the applique pieces are applied.

Wallhanging

Patricia Knoechel

24" square

Patricia Knoechel's Bridal Bouquet wallhanging has an assortment of flowers with ruched edges, yo yos, leaves and bias stems. The nosegay is made by arranging 2½" wide pre-gathered lace in a circle and placed in the upper right corner of a 16" background square of Kaufman's pastel pointillism dotted fabric. The flowers and stems may be hand or machine sewn in place. Arrange and sew a lightly stuffed, right handed glove under the nosegay lace. The sleeve is made from a flat bridal lace with scalloped edge, 8" wide by 10" long. Lightly gather at wrist, and turn under side edges before stitching in place. Embellish with buttons, pearls and ribbon. The butterfly is "fussy cut" from a Kaufman fabric. The border is cut at 4½" wide.

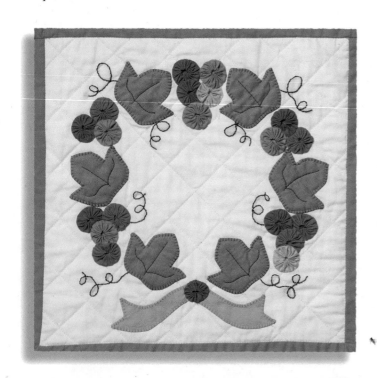

MATERIALS

PASTEL		DARK		APPLIQUE	FABRIC AMOUNT
	Orchid Amethyst Lilac		Purple Bright Periwinkle Amethyst	**Flat Grapes**	2" x 7" 3½" x 7" 3½" x 7" 7" x 9" cotton batting *Optional*
	Orchid Amethyst Lilac		Purple Bright Periwinkle Amethyst	**or Dimensional Grapes**	(4) circles with 3" diameter (7) circles with 3" diameter (8) circles with 3" diameter
	Sage		Alpine	**Leaves**	4½" x 7" 4½" x 7" cotton batting *Optional* 3½" x 17" 3½" x 17" cotton batting *Optional*
	#502		#501		DMC Pearl Cotton 3
	Woodrose		Plum	**Bow**	4" x 7"
	Amethyst		Eggplant	**Center of Bow**	(1) circle with 4" diameter

SEWING THE GRAPE WREATH

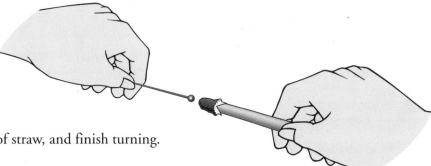

Trace pieces on Fusible Interfacing:

- ❖ six leaves
- ❖ flat grapes
- ❖ bow
- ❖ flat bow center

Sew pieces and trim. Clip inside points on leaves, and turn. *Optional* Lightly stuff flat grapes and leaves with cotton batting.

Turning Flat Grapes

1. Cut slit in center back of grape.
2. Insert wide straw in opening.
3. Push fabric into straw with bodkin. Do not push through straw.
4. Remove partially turned grape from end of straw, and finish turning.

Making Dimensional Grapes and Bow Center

Make yo yos from fabric circles. See page 22.

Stitching Vines

1. Place the 16" background square on placement sheet.
2. Trace vines. Extend ends of lines ½" under applique pieces.
3. Stitch on lines. Topstitch, (See page 18) couch (See page 46) or "chain stitch" (See page 16) with two strands of quilting thread or the pearl cotton.

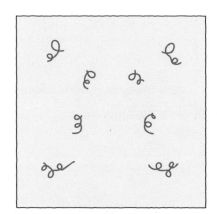

Finishing Leaves

1. Press in place. Finish outside edges.
2. Topstitch center of leaves with one of these methods:
    - ❖ heavy topstitching thread and long stitch
    - ❖ "chain stitch" with pearl cotton
    - ❖ "embroider" with thick thread from wrong side

"Embroidering" with Thick Threads

Pearl cotton, 100% Viscose thread, or ribbon thread can be used in the bobbin on some machines.

1. Wind the bobbin with selected heavy thread.
2. Use the "bobbin by-pass" or loosen your bobbin tension when placing the bobbin in the bobbin case.
3. Thread the upper machine with regular matching thread or invisible thread, and #70 needle.
4. From the wrong side, sew through the centers of the leaves.
5. Pull thread ends to wrong side and knot.

Finishing Flat Grapes

1. Press in place, overlapping as indicated.
2. Sew around with a straight stitch.
3. *Optional* From the wrong side, cut a small slit in center of grape. Lightly stuff using an orange stick.

Finishing Dimensional Yo yo Grapes

1. Pin in position.
2. Sew to background square by tacking center of each yo yo with invisible thread, or blind hem stitching around the outside edge.

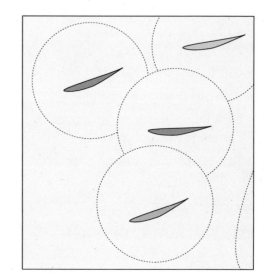

Finishing Bow

1. Press in place, and finish the outside edge.
2. Stitch around flat center, or tack yo yo center.

Wallhanging

Marcia Lasher

26" square

Marcia Lasher used her Elna 8000 to great advantage to enhance this Grape Wreath Wallhanging. She used the blanket stitch to applique the leaves with matching green thread. She used pattern #A-3 (triple stretch stitch) with a 3.7 stitch length to embroider the veins in the leaves. To embroider the vines she once again used the triple stretch stitch. She finished the block with some beautiful quilting using the #A-3 pattern stitch with a 2.5 length in a grape leaf and tendrils design and some outline quilting around the ribbon.

Mitering Borders

Pin 4" x 24" borders to the four sides, allowing the extra length to hang over equally on each end. Sew on the borders, beginning and ending the stitching exactly ¼" from the edge. On each corner, fold the quilt on the diagonal and match up the border strips with right sides together.

Fingerpress the seam allowance toward the quilt top to expose the stitching. Line up the 45° line on the 6" x 24" ruler with the border seam. Following the fold of the quilt and the 45° line, draw a diagonal line on the border extension. Beginning exactly at the ¼" point previously established, stitch on the line. Do not backstitch as you may need to pull out a stitch or two to enable the corner to lie flat.

Check the miter from the right side. Redo if necessary. Trim away the excess border ¼" from the stitched line. Repeat with all remaining border strips.

Add grapes and vines to the Grape Wreath border. The tiny yo yos were made from 1¼" circles.

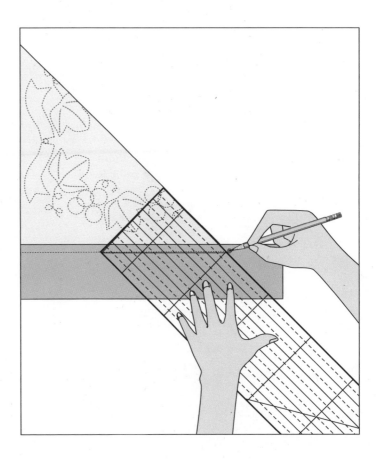

MATERIALS

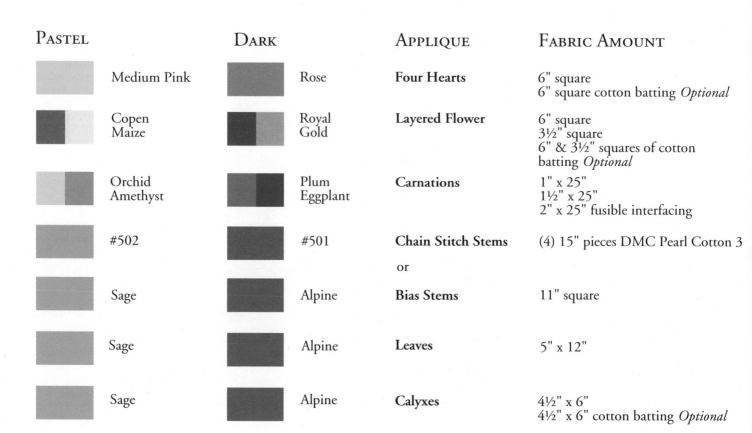

PASTEL		DARK		APPLIQUE	FABRIC AMOUNT
	Medium Pink		Rose	**Four Hearts**	6" square 6" square cotton batting *Optional*
	Copen Maize		Royal Gold	**Layered Flower**	6" square 3½" square 6" & 3½" squares of cotton batting *Optional*
	Orchid Amethyst		Plum Eggplant	**Carnations**	1" x 25" 1½" x 25" 2" x 25" fusible interfacing
	#502		#501	**Chain Stitch Stems** or	(4) 15" pieces DMC Pearl Cotton 3
	Sage		Alpine	**Bias Stems**	11" square
	Sage		Alpine	**Leaves**	5" x 12"
	Sage		Alpine	**Calyxes**	4½" x 6" 4½" x 6" cotton batting *Optional*

SEWING THE HEARTS & FLOWERS

Trace pieces on Fusible Interfacing:

- hearts
- layered flower
- leaves and calyxes

Sew pieces, trim, and turn following General Instructions.
Optional Lightly stuff hearts, calyxes, and layered flower.

Making Chain Stitch Stems

1. Lightly trace center lines on background square. Extend lines ½" on each end. See page 16.
2. "Chain stitch" on lines. Backstitch on ends, and trim pearl cotton.

Cutting Bias Stems

1. Line up 45° line on 6" x 24" ruler with edge of fabric. Cut. See pages 49 and 50.
2. Lining up ruler with the bias, cut three 1⅜" bias strips.

Making Bias Stems

1. Lightly trace stems on background fabric.
2. Sew 1⅜" bias strips with ¼" seam, regular thread on top, and fusing thread in bobbin. See pages 49 and 50.
3. Press with ⅜" wide bias bar. Trim seam to ⅛".
4. Cut four stems to 4" and fuse in place on background fabric.
5. Stitch in place with twin needle.

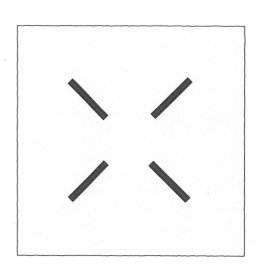

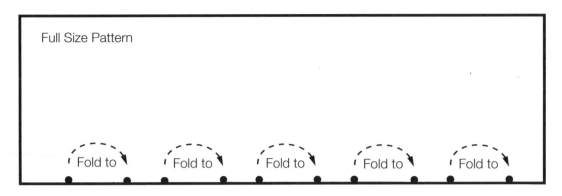

Full Size Pattern

Fold to Fold to Fold to Fold to Fold to

Making the Carnations

1. Sew two 25" strips together lengthwise. Press seam to darker side.

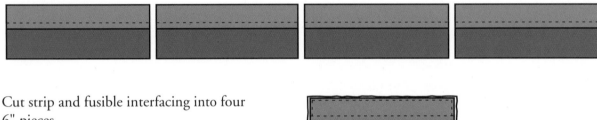

2. Cut strip and fusible interfacing into four 6" pieces.

3. Place interfacing with "dotted" fusible side right sides together to pieced strips.

4. With ¼" seam, sew three sides. Leave long side of dark fabric open.

5. Trim seams, clip corners, and turn.

6. Place piece on pattern and mark dots along bottom edge.

7. Fingerpress five pleats in place. Press onto a plain piece of paper to set pleats. Lift and press onto background square.

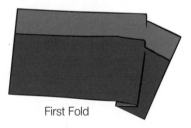

First Fold

Finished Carnation

8. Carefully lift up pressed carnation from plain paper, and press onto background fabric.

9. Press calyx overlapping bottom edge of carnation, and leaves.

10. Finish outside edges of leaves and calyxes as desired.

11. Sew carnations to background with blind hem stitch and invisible thread, or handstitch.

Adding the Layered Flower and Hearts

1. Layer flowers and hearts. Press in place.

2. Finish outside edges as desired.

Photo Album

Rhonda Rannow

Rhonda Rannow cleverly adapted the Hearts & Flowers pattern to cover a slant ring photo album. This technique could also be applied to other kinds of books.

Materials:
Album Size   11" x 12" x 2½"
Finished Block Size   9" (Reduced to 64% of pattern size)

- **Fabric to cover book**
  - (1) 14" x 26" piece
  - (2) 10" x 12" pieces
- **Fusible Fleece**
  - (2) 9" squares
  - (1) 12" x 24"
- **Wonder Under™**
  - (2) 10" x 12" pieces
- **Lightweight cardboard**
  - 2 pieces each approx. 9" x 11"
- **Glue gun**

Making the Block

Reduce block pattern to fit front of album/book--desired finished size. Follow instructions for block, adjusting sizes accordingly. Cut background fabric larger than the desired finished size so you can bring raw edges to back side. Cut a piece of fusible fleece the desired finished size and adhere to block, leaving approximately 1" around outside edge. Cut a piece of lightweight cardboard the desired finished size and attach block to it. Bring 1" excess fabric around and glue down outside edge to the back side.

Covering the Book

Use a purchased binder. Any of a variety of photo album styles will work. Cut fabric for outside of book larger than the size of the book.

Cut a piece of fusible fleece the size of book and center on wrong side of fabric. Lay this out with right side of fabric down, fusible fleece up, and opened book on top. Bring the 2" extra around to inside of book and adhere with a glue gun.

Measure the inside of book (each side) and cut out of lightweight cardboard. Cut fabric accordingly and adhere Wonder Under™ to the wrong side. Attach to cardboard. Using a glue gun, adhere to inside of book. Attach Block to the front of book with glue gun. Adorn with lace or whatever else you want.

MATERIALS

PASTEL		DARK		APPLIQUE	FABRIC AMOUNT
	Sage		Sage	**Two Holly Leaves**	3½" x 9" 3½" x 9" cotton batting *Optional*
	Sage		Alpine	**Four Holly Leaves**	4½" x 13" 4½" x 13" cotton batting *Optional*
	Woodrose Blush Pink Plum		Crimson Plum Dusty Pink	**Berries**	(3) circles with 1¾" diameter (3) circles with 1¾" diameter (3) circles with 1¾" diameter
	Blush Pink		Plum	**Doves**	5½" x 6½" 5½" x 6½" cotton batting *Optional*
	Medium Pink		Rose	**Wings**	3" x 4½" 3" x 4½" cotton batting *Optional*
	Plum		Crimson	**Heart**	2" square
	Woodrose		Rose	**Bow**	5" x 6½"

Optional (2) small beads
for doves' eyes

SEWING THE HOLLY WREATH

Trace pieces on Fusible Interfacing:

- ❖ holly leaves
- ❖ doves and wings
- ❖ heart
- ❖ bow

Sew pieces, trim, and turn, following General Instructions.

Optional Stuff holly leaves, doves, and wings.

Arranging the Pieces

1. Place pieces on the 16" background square. Place wings on the birds. Tuck the ends of the bow under the holly.

2. Press in place.

3. Finish the outside edges.

4. Topstitch centers of holly leaves. Sew eyes to doves with optional beads or colonial knots. See page 26.

Making the Berries

1. With quilting thread in the bobbin, machine baste around the outside edges of the 1¾" circles. Leave the threads long.

2. Place a small "berry size" wad of batting in the center of each circle.

3. Pull on the bobbin threads and gather the circle around the batting.

4. Knot. Do not trim the threads.

5. Position each berry, and hand sew to the background square with the basting threads.

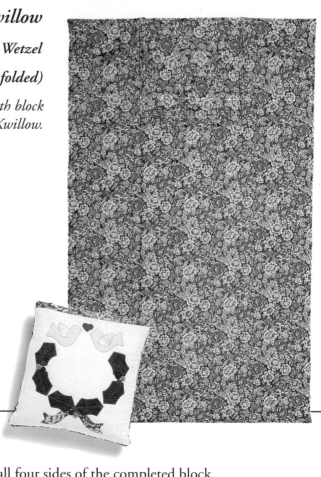

Kwillow

Pat Wetzel

43" x 70" (17½" x 18½" folded)

Pat Wetzel cleverly turned the Holly Wreath block into a beautiful and useful Kwillow.

Materials

- ❖ **One completed 16" block**
- ❖ **Lightweight (3 oz.) bonded batting**
    18½" square for pillow lining
    48" x 72"
- ❖ **2 skeins embroidery floss**
- ❖ **Quilt fabric**   2 yards
- ❖ **Quilt backing** 2¾ yards
    Cut into   (1) 18½" square
              (2) 1½" x 45" strips
              (1) 45" x 72" rectangle

Instructions

Lining the Pillow Front

1. Sew a 1½" border strip to all four sides of the completed block.

2. Place the completed quilt block right sides together to the 18½" fabric square. Place the lightweight batting square on the bottom of the two.

3. Stitch around the outside edge on three sides, leaving the bottom edge open.

4. Trim away the excess batting. Turn right side out.

5. Machine quilt by "stitching in the ditch" with invisible thread around the applique and borders.

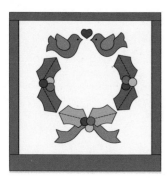

Layering the Kwillow

1. Lay out the lightweight batting.

2. Lay the quilt backing on top of the batting, with right side up.

3. Place the pillow front to the right side of the backing, matching up the bottom toward the raw edge.

   The front side of the pillow will be inside the pocket when it is used as a quilt. It will be on the outside of the pocket when it is used as a pillow.

4. Place the quilt fabric right sides together to the backing, with the lined pillow front in place on one end.

5. Trim the edges straight. Pin around the outside edge.

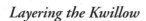

Wallhanging

Carol Neumann

Sue Bouchard

Jan Petersen

27" square

Carol Neumann made this festive Holly Wreath Wallhanging, with Jan Petersen doing the quilting and Sue Bouchard adding the binding.

Carol framed the wallhanging with a 1½" border, then added colorful sprigs of holly to 4¾" corner squares and borders.

Finishing the Kwillow

1. Stitch around the outside edge, leaving a 12" opening in the middle of one side.
2. Trim away the excess batting. Trim the corners.
3. Turn right side out through the opening.
4. Slipstitch the opening shut.
5. Smooth out all layers.
6. Tie all layers together with a surgeon's square knot approximately every 6".
7. Pin the pillow flap in place with the patchwork right sides to the quilt fabric.
8. Edgestitch along the two sides, reinforcing the stress points. See detail.
9. Topstitch around the outside edge of the kwillow.

Folding the Quilt into the Pillow

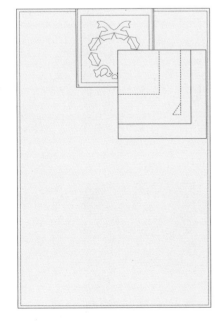

1. Lay the quilt with the pocket underneath. Fold into thirds lengthwise.

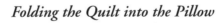

2. Fold in fourths toward the pocket.

3. Pull the pillow right side out over the folds.

FINISHING

Garden Maze Setting

For sewing twelve blocks together in the
Garden Maze setting, you need:

Thirty-one lattice
and twenty cornerstones.

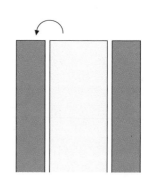

To check the accuracy of your seam width, make one lattice and one cornerstone following the directions. Pin and sew together. Check to see that they match. If they don't match, make an adjustment in your seam allowance.

Sewing the Strips for Thirty-one Lattice

1. Lay out two stacks of 1½" medium strips and one stack of 3" light background strips in this order:

    Place sixteen strips in each stack.

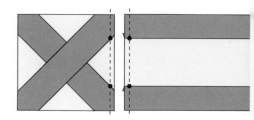

2. Flip the light background strip right sides together to the medium strip. **Sew with a scant ¼" seam allowance (¼" less two threads)** and fifteen stitches per inch.

3. Stop and measure seam. Make adjustment if necessary.

4. Flip the second medium strip right sides together to the medium/background strip.

5. Assembly-line sew.

6. Set the seams with the medium on top. Lift and press the seams toward the medium.

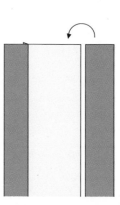

Cutting the Lattice Strips

1. Layer several strips on a gridded cutting mat. Extend the left selvage ends to the left of zero.

2. Trim at zero, squaring off the end.

3. Cut into 16" block size lattice pieces. Cut a total of thirty-one.

4. Measure the width of the strips. They should measure 5".

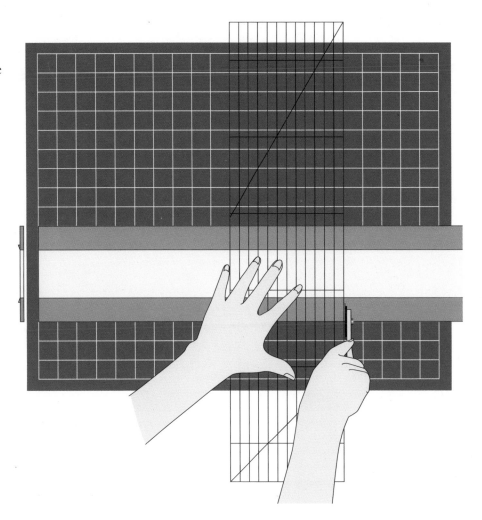

Sewing the Pieces for Twenty Cornerstones

1. In piles of forty, lay out background triangles with 2" x 3½" medium rectangles.

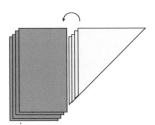

2. Flip a triangle onto a 3½" side, right sides together, matching top edges. Assembly-line sew. Do not clip apart.

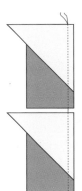

3. Repeat, sewing remaining triangles to other side of rectangle. Match straight edges of triangles.

4. Press seams toward rectangle.

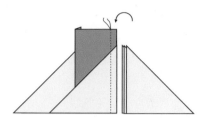

5. In piles of twenty, lay out these pieces with the 2" x 7½" rectangles.

6. Flip the right piece to the rectangle, and center.

7. Assembly-line sew.

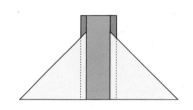

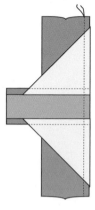

8. Flip the second piece to the rectangle, carefully lining up seams.

9. Assembly line sew.

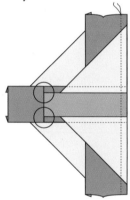

10. From the wrong side, press seams toward the rectangle.

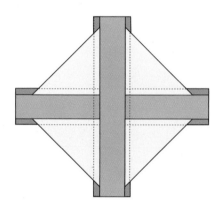

Squaring Up Each Piece

1. Place the block with the long strip pointing to the left.

2. Place the 6" ruler on the block with its diagonal line centered, and the 2" and 3" squaring lines matching the seams.

3. Center the 2½" squaring line on the ruler with the center of the block.

4. Trim two sides.

5. Turn block around and trim remaining two sides, squaring to 5".

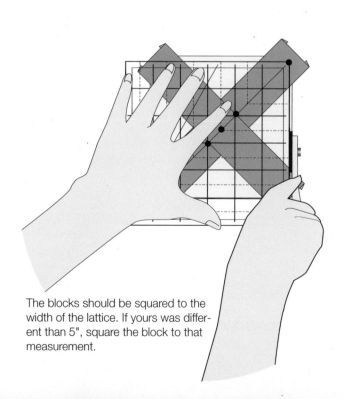

The blocks should be squared to the width of the lattice. If yours was different than 5", square the block to that measurement.

wing the Garden Maze Top Together

1. Lay out the applique blocks, stripped lattice, and
   mazed cornerstones in rows. Check that the long
   strip in the cornerstone is consistently turned in
   the same direction.

2. On the top row, flip the lattice and block right sides together to the cornerstone and lattice.

3. Pin and match the seams on the lattice with the seams on the cornerstones, ¼" from the edges.

4. Assembly-line sew the pieces together. Backstitch at the beginning and end. Do not clip the threads between the pieces.

5. Assembly-line sew the third cornerstone and lattice to the second. Continue until all lattice and blocks in the first row are sewn together.

6. Flip the top lattice row right sides together to the block and lattice.

7. At the cornerstones, where the pieces are joined by threads, pin and match the seams carefully. Push the seams in opposite directions toward the lattice.

8. Sew each row together.

9. Sew the rows together into one top.

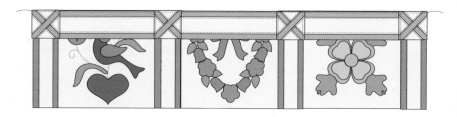

Check the Fit

If you want a larger quilt, lay the quilt top on your bed before adding the borders and backing. Measure to find how much border you need to get the fit you want. Keep in mind, the quilt will "shrink" approximately 2" in length and width after completion of machine quilting.

Sewing the Lattice and Cornerstones Top Together

1. Lay out the applique blocks, 3" x 16" lattice
   pieces, and 3" cornerstones in rows.

2. On the top row, flip the lattice and block right sides together to the cornerstone and lattice.

3. Assembly-line sew the pieces together. Backstitch at the beginning and end. Do not clip the threads between the pieces.

4. Assembly-line the third cornerstone and lattice to the second. Continue until the row is sewn together.

5. Flip the top lattice row right sides together to the blocks and lattice.

6. At the cornerstones, where the pieces are joined by threads, match the seams carefully. Push the seams in opposite directions toward the lattice.

7. Sew the rows together.

8. Sew the rows together into one top.

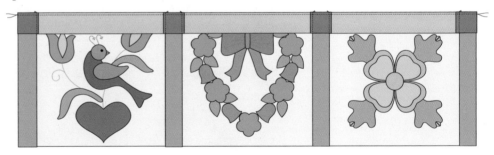

Check the Fit

If you want a larger quilt, lay the quilt top on your bed before adding the borders and backing. Measure to find how much border you need to get the fit you want. Keep in mind, the quilt will "shrink" approximately 2" in length and width after completion of machine quilting.

Adding an Optional Framing Border and/or Outside Border to Make a Larger Quilt

If you want the quilt top to "frame" the mattress, and the top does not reach the edges, add a framing border before the mitered border. An outside border can also be added after the mitered border to get the fit you want.

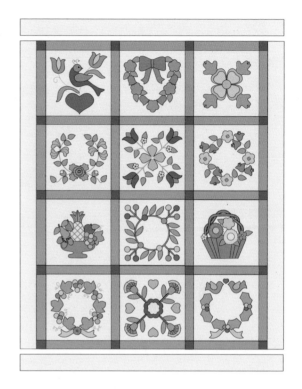

1. Square off the selvage edges, and sew strips together lengthwise.
2. Measure the long sides of the quilt.
3. Cut two pieces the same length from the border fabric.
4. Pin the borders to the long sides.
5. Stitch from end to end. Fold them out flat.
6. Measure the short sides of the quilt from one outside edge to the other, including the first long borders.
7. Cut two borders that measurement.
8. Pin the borders to the short sides.
9. Stitch. Fold them out flat.

Making a Floral Border with Mitered Corners

The pattern is designed to fit a 16" background square in either a Garden Maze or Lattice and Cornerstone setting. Regardless of the number of blocks used in the quilt, the pattern can be adjusted to fit. The corners are bows that will adapt to fit your choice of framing border or no framing border.

You need this many pieces for a twelve block quilt:

- ❖ 32 five petal flowers
- ❖ 56 bell flowers (28 each of two different fabrics)
- ❖ 56 buds
- ❖ 64 leaves for five petal flowers
- ❖ 56 leaves for bell flowers
- ❖ 4 corner bows
- ❖ 14 bias strips

The floral pattern pieces are the same ones used in President's Wreath. See page 40.

1. Trace 8 sets of President's Wreath patterns, plus 56 additional leaves.
2. Fold and press the (56) 2" squares into buds.
3. Sew pieces, trim, and turn following General Instructions.
4. Trace and sew 4 bows, using the pattern from Sweetheart Wreath. See page 24.
5. Sew bias strips with fusing thread in bobbin and ¼" seam. See pages 49 and 50. Press and trim.

Sewing the Vines

1. Lay the quilt out on a large table or floor area. Yours may or may not have a framing border.

2. Place the 10" wide border strips around the outside edge of the quilt, centering strips to sides. Strips should extend at least 11" at each end for mitered corners.

3. Place the pattern under the center of the bottom border strip. Line up the center of the block with the center of the placement sheet. Note the positioning of the inside and outside edges of the placement sheet.

4. Trace the curved line on the border strip. Mark the placement for each five petal flower with two dashed lines. These lines will be used later for repositioning the placement sheet.

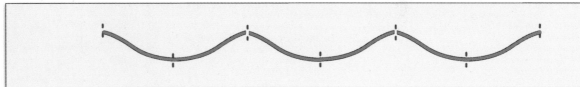

5. Slide the pattern along to each block and mark the curved lines and five petal flower placement lines.

6. Press the bias strips on the curved lines. Trim the ends to fit.

7. Stitch down the vines with a twin needle and matching thread.

Sewing the Floral Pieces

1. Place the pattern sheet on the ironing board. Working on one block at a time, position each piece on the border strip.

2. Tuck the buds in the bell flowers. Press.

3. Roll the borders from the ends to make the long pieces easy to manage. Pin or clamp.

4. Sew around the outside edges of each piece as desired. The easiest applique technique is using invisible thread and a blindhem stitch.

5. Repeat with each block.

Sewing the Mitered Border Strips

Sew the border strips to the quilt and miter the corners. See page 79.

Adding the Corners

1. Press the four corner bows in place.

2. The easiest way to applique the bows is by hand. Turn to page 80, Layering the Quilt.

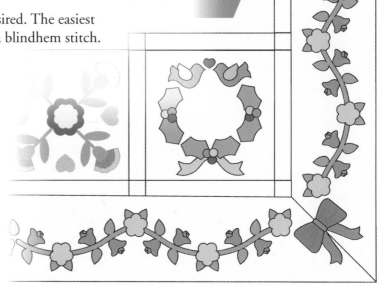

Making a Scalloped Border with Mitered Corners

You need this many pieces for a twelve block quilt:

- ❖ 14 side scallops
- ❖ 4 corner scallops
- ❖ 18 five petal flowers (President's Wreath, page 40)
- ❖ 28 leaves (President's Wreath, page 40)

Choose one of these methods for duplicating the patterns:

- ❖ trace directly on fusible interfacing
- ❖ transfer patterns to fabric

Tracing Patterns on Fusible Interfacing

1. Trace the patterns. Glue patterns to cardboard or cut from template plastic.

2. Trace around the patterns with a permanent pen on the smooth side of the fusible interfacing.

3. Group same pieces until you have the number needed of each.

4. Cut the fabric for the scallops in half lengthwise to fit the 22" wide fusible interfacing.

5. Place each fusible piece on its fabric piece, with the dotted fusible side to the right side of the fabric.

Transferring Patterns to Fabric

1. Trace and cut the pattern sheet apart. Do not trim around each piece.

2. Trace each pattern with a transferable pen.

3. Place the paper pattern on the wrong side of the appropriate fabric. Press with steam until the pattern transfers to the fabric.

4. Move the pattern and repeat. You will need to retrace the pattern after several transfers.

5. Place the right side of the fabric to the dotted fusible side of the interfacing.

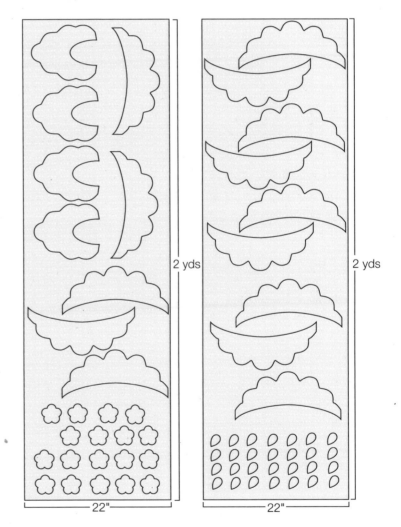

2 yds

2 yds

22"   22"

Sewing Around the Pieces

1. Sew on the inside edge of the line on each piece.

2. Trim, and clip curves on scallops.

3. Cut a small turning hole in the interfacing, and turn right side out. Gently curve the outside edges.

Sewing Side Scallops to Four Strips

1. Lay the quilt on a large table or floor area.

2. Place the 10" border strips around the edge of the quilt, centering strips to sides. Strips should extend at least 11" at each end. The excess is provided for the mitered corners.

3. Place the side scallops on the 10" borders. Line them up 1" from the inside edge and 2" from the outside edge. Place so the space between the scallops lines up with the cornerstones.

4. Pin scallops in place. Carry border strips to the iron.

5. Press.

6. Finish outside edges of scallops as desired.

7. Press five petal flowers and leaves in place.

8. Finish flowers and leaves as desired.

Sewing the Mitered Border Strips

Sew the borders to the quilt and miter the corners. See page 79.

Adding the Corners

1. Press and sew corner scallops to the corners of the quilt.

2. Add corner flowers and leaves. The easiest way to finish is by hand.

Mitering Strips to Quilt

1. Pin the long borders to the two sides, allowing the extra length to hang over equally on each end.

2. Sew on the borders, beginning and ending the stitching exactly ¼" from the edge.

3. Pin and sew the short borders to each side, beginning and ending the stitching ¼" from the edge.

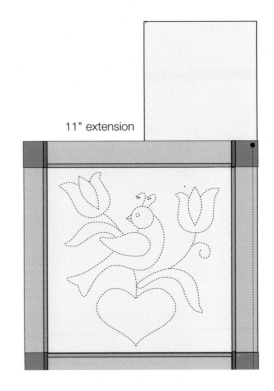

11" extension

4. On each corner, fold the quilt on the diagonal and carefully match up the border strips with right sides together.

5. Fingerpress the seam allowance toward the quilt top to expose the stitching.

6. Line up the 45° line on the 6" x 24" ruler with the border seam.

7. Following the fold of the quilt and the 45° line, draw a diagonal line on the border extension.

8. Beginning exactly at the ¼" point previously established, stitch on the line. Do not backstitch as you may need to pull out a stitch or two to enable the corner to lie flat.

9. Check the miter from the right side. Redo if necessary.

10. Trim away the excess border ¼" from the stitched line.

11. Repeat with remaining border strips.

12. Press mitered seams opened.

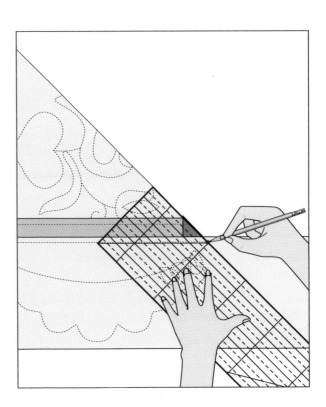

Layering the Quilt

1. Spread out the backing on a large table or floor area with the right side down. Clamp the fabric to the edge of the table with binder clips or tape the backing to the floor.

2. Layer the batting on top of the backing.

3. With the quilt top right side up, center on the backing. Smooth until all layers are flat. Clamp or tape outside edges.

4. Safety pin the layers together every three to five inches through the lattice, borders, and center of the blocks. Use a pinning tool to assist the process

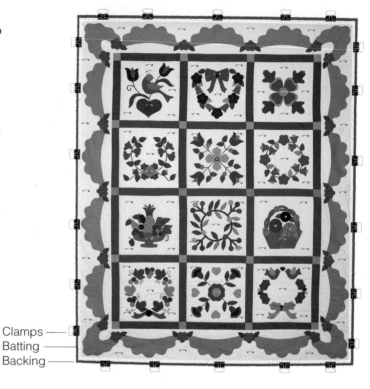

Clamps ——
Batting ——
Backing ——

Machine Quilting Your Top

The ideal machine quilting area is where the sewing machine bed is level with the table, and there is a large area to the left of the machine to support the quilt. Machine quilt on a day when you are relaxed to help avoid muscle strain down your neck, shoulders, and back. Sit in a raised stenographer's chair so your arms can rest on the table.

"Stitch in the Ditch" along the Lattice (Lattice and Cornerstone or Garden Maze Setting)

1. Thread your machine with matching thread or invisible thread. If you use invisible thread, loosen your top tension. Match the bobbin thread to the backing.

2. Attach your walking foot, and lengthen the stitch to 8 to 10 stitches per inch.

3. Roll the top and bottom to the center lattice. Clip the rolls in place.

4. Spread the lattice seams open, and "stitch in the ditch."

5. Unroll the quilt, and roll the sides to the center lattice. Clip the rolls in place, and "stitch in the ditch."

6. Continue to unroll and roll the quilt until all the lattice is stitched, anchoring the blocks.

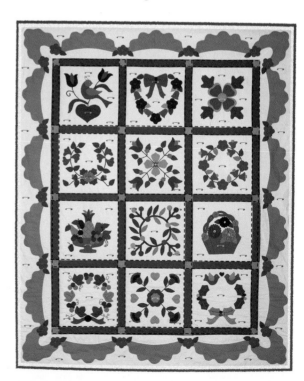

Free Motion Machine Quilting

The easiest way to quilt the blocks is by free motion machine quilting around each piece either "in the ditch" or ¼" away.

Refer to your instruction manual for directions on how to darn with your machine. Use a darning foot or spring needle, and drop the feed dogs or cover with a plate.

No stitch length is required as you control the length. Use a fine needle and a little hole throat plate with a center needle position. Use invisible or regular thread in the top and regular thread to match the backing in the bobbin. Loosen the top tension if using invisible thread.

If you are a novice at this technique, imperfections are easily hidden by using invisible thread and "stitching in the ditch" around each piece to add dimension.

Free motion quilting ¼" away from each piece with thread matching the background is traditional looking, but more challenging.

1. Bring the bobbin thread up on the edge of the applique, or ¼" away. Lower the needle into the background fabric and drop the foot. Moving the fabric very slowly, take a few tiny stitches to lock them. Snip off the tails of the threads.

2. With your eyes watching the outline of the block ahead of the needle, and your fingertips stretching the fabric and acting as a quilting hoop, move the fabric in a steady motion while the machine is running at a constant speed. Keep the top of the quilt in the same position by moving the fabric underneath the needle side to side, and forward and backward.

3. Lock off the tiny stitches and clip the threads at the end of the block.

Free Motion Stippling

Free motion stippling is an overall meandering design. Because it is "free form," marking is not necessary. The machine set up and technique are the same as free motion quilting, but the background is "filled" with meandering stitches.

Set up a practice swatch of the three layers to become comfortable with moving the fabric to make your desired size stitch. Adjust the tension for either invisible or regular thread. Practice moving your hands back and forward and sideways, but not turning the swatch. The only requirements for stippling are not to sew across a stippled line of stitching or across the applique.

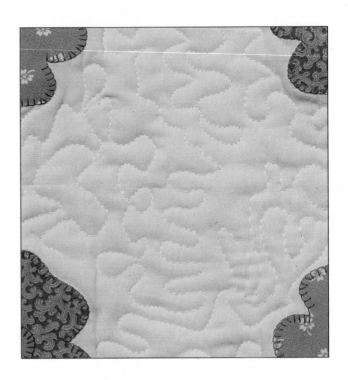

Cross Hatch Quilting Each Block

This is a traditional quilted finish for an applique block. While it looks easy, there is considerable time involved because the ends of each stitching line must be locked with backstitching.

1. Set up your machine with a walking foot, thread to match the background on top, and thread to match the backing in the bobbin.

2. With a silver pencil or chalk, lightly draw diagonal lines from corner to corner. Do not mark on the applique pieces.

3. Draw diagonal lines evenly spaced 2" apart from the center diagonal lines in both directions.

4. Sew the center diagonals first, backstitching and locking the stitches on the outside edges of the block and applique pieces. Do not stitch over the applique.

5. Sew on all diagonal lines and trim threads.

Adding the Binding

Use a walking foot attachment and regular thread on top and in the bobbin to match the binding.

1. Square off the selvage edges, and sew strips together lengthwise.

2. Fold and press in half with wrong sides together.

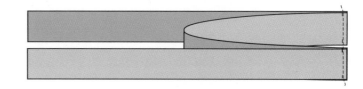

3. Line up the raw edges of the folded binding with the raw edges of the quilt in the middle of one side.

4. Begin stitching 4" from the end of the binding.

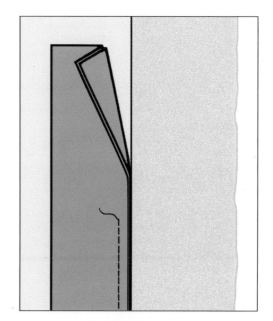

5. At the corner, stop the stitching ¼" from the edge with the needle in the fabric. Raise the presser foot and turn the quilt to the next side. Put the foot back down.

6. Stitch backwards ¼" to the edge of the binding, raise the foot, and pull the quilt forward slightly.

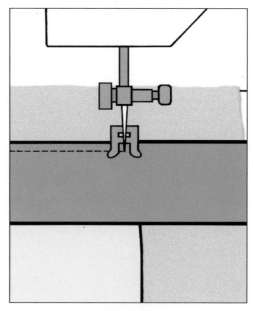

7. Fold the binding strip straight up on the diagonal. Fingerpress the diagonal fold.

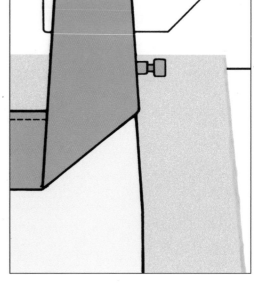

8. Fold the binding strip straight down with the diagonal fold underneath. Line up the top of the fold with the raw edge of the binding underneath.

9. Begin sewing from the edge.

10. Continue stitching and mitering the corners around the outside of the quilt.

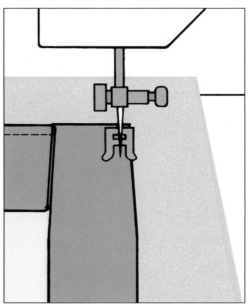

11. Stop stitching 4" from where the ends will overlap.

12. Line up the two ends of binding. Trim the excess with a ½" overlap.

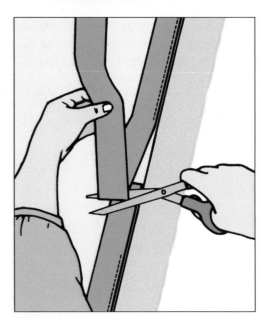

13. Open out the folded ends and pin right sides together. Sew a ¼" seam.

14. Continue to stitch the binding in place.

15. Trim the batting and backing up to the raw edges of the binding.

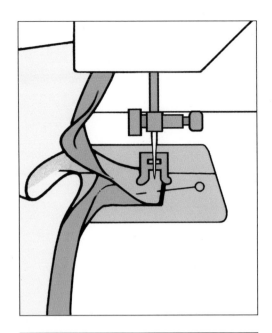

16. Fold the binding to the back side of the quilt. Pin in place so that the folded edge on the binding covers the stitching line. Tuck in the excess fabric at each miter on the diagonal.

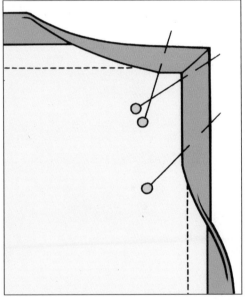

17. From the right side, "stitch in the ditch" using invisible thread on the front side, and a bobbin thread to match the binding on the back side. Catch the folded edge of the binding on the back side with the stitching.

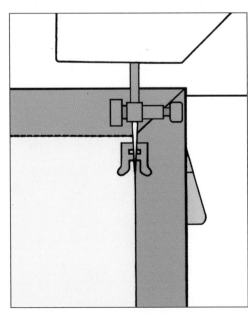

Index

ORDER INFORMATION

Quilt in a Day books offer a wide range of techniques and are directed toward a variety of skill levels. If you do not have a quilt shop in your area, you may write for a complete catalog and current price list of all books and patterns published by Quilt in a Day®, Inc., 1955 Diamond Street, San Marcos, CA 92069 or call 1-619-591-0929 or order toll free 1-800-825-9458.

Easy

These books are easy enough for beginners of any age.
Log Cabin Quilt in a Day
Irish Chain
Bits & Pieces
Trip Around the World
Heart's Delight
Scrap Quilt
Rail Fence
Dresden Placemats
Flying Geese
Star for all Seasons
Winning Hand

Applique

While these books offer a variety of techniques, easy applique is featured in each.
Dresden Plate
Sunbonnet Sue Visits Quilt in a Day
Recycled Treasures
Creating with Color
Spools & Tools

Intermediate to Advanced

With a little Quilt in a Day experience, these books offer a rewarding project.
Trio of Treasured Quilts
Lover's Knot
Amish Quilt
May Basket
Morning Star
Friendship Quilt
Tulip Quilt
Burgoyne Surrounded
Bird's Eye
Snowball
Tulip Table Runner

Holiday

When a favorite holiday is approaching, Quilt in a Day is there to help you plan.
Country Christmas
Bunnies & Blossoms
Patchwork Santa
Last Minute Gifts
Angel of Antiquity
Log Cabin Wreath
Log Cabin Tree
Country Flag
Lover's Knot Placemats

Sampler

Always and forever popular are books with a variety of patterns.
The Sampler
Block Party Series 1, Quilter's Year
Block Party Series 2, Baskets and Flowers
Block Party Series 3, Quilters' Almanac
Block Party Series 4, Christmas Traditions
Block Party Series 5, Pioneer Sampler

Angle Piecing

Quilt in a Day "template free" methods make angle cutting less of a challenge.
Diamond Log Cabin
Pineapple Quilt
Blazing Star Tablecloth
Schoolhouse
Radiant Star

Love

Your unique qualities and contributions are recognized and deeply appreciated.

Acknowledgements

Innocence

Grant and Orion Burns, who share my Garden

Devotion

Merritt Voigtlander, Debbie Smith, Susan Sells, Nancy Loftis, and Loretta Smith, the Beautifiers of this publication

Durability

Quilt in a Day Staff, peacemakers of incredible strength and fortitude

Healing

for Janet

Cynthia Martin, who graciously machine quilted the four cover applique quilts

Charity

Patricia Knoechel, who helped design and sew the cover quilts

Sweet Character

Quiltmakers who willingly designed and made the beautiful featured projects

Gratitude

Quilt in a Day Block Party Ladies, the pattern testers

Delight

Quilt in a Day "Strippers" who Bloom into Appliquers

Good Luck